Building The Expo

Saving Innovation From Its
Underwhelming & Overused Past

Daniel Maycock

Introduction by Dr. Al Erisman

DEDICATED TO MY WIFE, TRACY

CONTENTS

ACKNOWLEDGMENTS

I'd like to extend my deepest thanks to the friends, coworkers, and family that helped make this book possible. This book wouldn't be possible without each of you helping to take this from an idea to reality.

Introduction

Imagine you are talking with a new person in the office, and discover you live in the same neighborhood. Now suppose a few days later that you start out for work and see your neighbor and business colleague in the car ahead of you. At the first intersection, he turns right where you usually turn left. You assume he is stopping off somewhere before work, so you turn left as usual. To your surprise, when you arrive at the office you see him there, already halfway through his first cup of coffee. He obviously discovered a better route to the office. How could this happen?

In fact, this scenario is played out daily in every business, not just in finding the way to work. We develop a process for doing something, and then it becomes a habit and we don't think much more about it. In businesses today, processes are even embedded in computer software, and few know what the process is or why it was adopted in the first place. It often takes an outside event, or a new person's question, to prompt the reexamination of the process.

There was a time at Boeing when the EPA required the company to stop using a particular cleaning agent. The immediate concern raised in the company was the new cleaning process, whatever it was, would be more expensive, with a possible hit on quality and finish. Because of the outside regulation, people got to work on a systematic study to find a new way. The result (it doesn't always happen this way) was a better solution, no environmental impact, and lower cost. If this was the result, why wasn't the change made before the regulation? There was no driving force to do so, people were comfortable with the old process, and there were lots of other things to do.

A big challenge for today's businesses comes from technology. Because of its rapid change, almost every day technology enables a better process or product, or even opens the possibility of a potential customer or competitor. Old habits die hard. And unlike the simple scenario about the route to work, often the new way of doing things is disruptive. It is not just a matter of taking a different set of streets to the office. It is a change that ripples through the organization with secondary impacts. It is a change that may lead to reorganizations and learning new ways to doing things. It may undermine my own position of authority and responsibility. These changes are much harder.

For many years I had responsibility for a research lab at The Boeing Company focused on information technology and mathematics. We were responsible for understanding and identifying new technology and mathematical research that could make a difference for the company. The goal was to create change that could come to the company from our technical areas. To do this required having our technical people themselves working at the new frontiers, often contributing to research knowledge.

For many colleagues leading research in other companies, good research and recognition in the technical community was the goal. We also had some great people in our lab who did just that. But that was just the start. They also needed to understand the context of the company and where and how the new ideas could bring benefit to the company. The ultimate measure was helping the company create new products, new processes, save money, and save time. We justified our existence every year by the value the company saw as measured by those in engineering who designed the new products; by those in manufacturing who built the new product; by those in customer services who supported the products once they were delivered; and by our many other "customers" throughout the company. The value came when the new ideas were implemented and made a positive difference they could measure.

We could not do our work by simply asking our customers what they wanted. Since they were not aware of what was happening in the world of research, they could only ask for things in terms of what they thought they could get. Further, if we provided only what they were asking for, we could perhaps supply great value only to realize at a later point that a competitor had a much better solution to the same problem.

The immersion of our people in the technical community required one more thing that brought great benefits. It required that our people contribute to the state of the art in their fields. It was not enough to keep up with the latest ideas through journals, attending conferences, or meeting with vendors. These things were necessary, of course. But by contributing to the state of the art the people had a seat at the table, developed collaborations with other researchers and vendors. In this way future technology was shaped by the problems that Boeing found important. In fact, others carried out the more basic research through independent funding, and this ultimately also brought value to Boeing.

The remaining challenge is to take the good ideas developed through this process and get them implemented in the company, since that is the ultimate goal. While the process described to this point is something we did in our lab, the next step is common with many others. A vendor develops a product often starting with a deep understanding of the market, and wants to get it sold to the company. A consultant works with the company on a project and wants to create a success. A technical person in the organization sees a new approach and believes it will help in his or her career by making a difference for the company. This next step to implementation and realizing the benefits is often very hard indeed. Often we found ourselves working in partnership with a vendor (or multiple vendor) solution, and in cooperation with an inside person motivated to make the change.

No one should believe that because you have a great

idea, it will immediately be embraced. Part of the problem here is change, even in the simplest of circumstances. Heifetz and Linsky argue in their book Leadership on the Line (2002), "People cannot see at the beginning of the adaptive process that the new situation will be any better than the current condition. What they do see clearly is the potential for loss," p. 13. Even the best and simplest ideas can be rejected and fail to deliver value. The challenge at this point is to sort out whether the resistance is real (it is really a bad idea when all of the details are accounted for), or if it is simply a desire to keep things as they are. The simpler it is to take out the old and plug in the new the more likely it is you can get to value, though even here it may take some effort. Unfortunately, the simpler the change often the smaller the value, as I will develop later.

I remember when PCs were introduced for office use in the early 1980s. My secretary came to me and said, "These PCs are for younger people. I want to keep my typewriter." She was incredibly valuable to the organization, and she was also incredibly determined. A delicate situation indeed, one that is often the case when new technology is brought to an organization.

I asked her to spend a few hours once a week simply experimenting with the PC under the tutelage of a woman who had significant expertise and significant humility (both important). I promised her that after four such sessions, she could tell me she didn't want a PC, and she would be able to keep her typewriter. At a break after the first two hours on the first day, she came into my office and stated emphatically, "I have to have one of those PCs on my desk." Problem solved. All we were trying to accomplish in the first round was to use the PC for word processing. No shared documents. No network. No spread sheets. These all came later. The benefit to her was no retyped documents, or trying to make a change in a page to avoid having changes ripple through the document. She basically was able to do her old job more efficiently; no new work was required other than learning the commands to create the document.

Most new technology is more far-reaching than that. A

new accounts payable system may enable doing the work of 100 people with only 5 people. In addition to many people losing their jobs, the boss of the organization may lose his executive position. A new enterprise system for a company can fundamentally restructure processes throughout the company, decrease the number of people needed for the work, and lead to entirely different organizational structures. Most enterprise systems implementations fail. A mathematical model for supply chain management we had developed in 1992 finally was implemented, with great savings for the company, in 1997. This kind of change is difficult. More than 20 years ago, Michael Hammer argued that if we use technology to simply automate what we used to do, too often the result is higher costs and minimal value. His Harvard Business Review paper, "Reengineering Work: Don't Automate, Obliterate," made this point in 1990. Soon after 1990, productivity results for the use of information technology finally started to show up in the measures as the world woke up to this key point. It should also be clear why this kind of change is so much more difficult to achieve.

I could offer countless stories of technological change efforts in Boeing that encountered precisely this type of difficulty. And as I have consulted with other companies, the story is magnified. We began to recognize and use a formula for change: D*V*F must be greater than I. In words, Dissatisfaction with present circumstances, Vision for a better future, and First steps that seem clear and possible must be greater than the inertia of staying where you are. In the supply chain example mentioned earlier, the V and the F had been laid out in 1992. But in 1997 a significant increase in production started to cause difficulty in delivery. The dissatisfaction from not being able to deliver airplanes is what drove the implementation. Sometimes there is a political factor in blocking the implementation of innovation as well. Both government and business can play this game, and it is over and above the other reasons discussed. Another friend worked in an electronics company and was responsible for the implementation of an enterprise system there using vendor A. Six months into the implementation, his project was on time and within budget, a true miracle in enterprise system implementations, when the project was cancelled. It had nothing to do with the technology. It turned out a leader in the company really wanted to use vendor B, and the project was being carried out to force a better price in the negotiation with vendor B. The legitimate resistance to change comes in two flavors, and the more complex the implementation, the more difficult it is to distinguish between the two.

Is the resistance because the new technology is truly a bad idea? It may solve one problem and create three more. It may be too early because the technology is not as reliable as it needs to be. It may have more subtle implications. Too much cockpit automation for pilots may result in boredom and inattention, making it difficult to respond in times when the pilot is needed. This same scenario is played out in hospital automation, manufacturing processes, and countless other areas.

Or is the resistance because the person doesn't want to do the new thing? This may be out of fear of the loss of a job or position. It may be because the person is simply comfortable with the old way. It may be because the person lacks confidence in the new technology. It takes great wisdom to discern between the two.

The CFO of a large software company told me the story of his own resistance during an enterprise system implementation. He found that the new software would not give him the old information from which he made decisions, so he told the president they would have to make some changes in the software to accommodate his needs. The big challenge in making changes to vendor supplied software is managing these changes as new versions are delivered from the vendor. How do these new changes get made, can they even work with the new version, etc.? The president was aware of these issues and had said there would be no changes to the vendor supplied software. When confronted with the demand for the change, the president said, "We are not going to change the software, so I guess that means I need to get a new CFO." My friend said he quickly figured out how to do his job with the existing software. Often, however, understanding whether the adaptation will truly cause a problem, or can be overcome, is much more difficult than this.

Finding the way to success through the maze of technology insertion challenges is part technical, part psychological, part determination. It will continue to be a significant challenge.

This brings me to Dan Maycock's book. When Dan and I first began talking about this subject, he offered a set of ideas for addressing the challenges of inserting new technology. Basically, I realized that he had identified an approach that recognizes many of the pitfalls I had seen in this process, and carves a path to technology insertion that addresses these pitfalls. It doesn't mean that reading this book will make putting new technology into your company an easy, pain-free experience. That won't happen. But it will help a great deal.

One of his big ideas is to recognize that the first approach (inserting the technology with minimal change) is easier than the second, and perhaps the second harder problem can be addressed by starting with the first. Not as much value will be achieved by following a minimal disruption insertion of the technology at the beginning. But it is like the camel in the tent. Once it is in, it can be expanded and grown from there. While it may seem like a longer path, in reality it may be much shorter with much less grief.

Dr. Al Erisman
Director of Technology, The Boeing Company (retired)

1
WHAT IS INNOVATION?

My consulting career began while I was working for a team that was trying to break out of traditional consulting and introduce new types of offerings to our company. To be branded as an R&D group without using the R&D term though, and present ourselves in the most profitable light possible, we needed to appear both innovative and productive at the same time. Several of us worked together in a pod, while a handful of others were out selling. The challenge was how to appear innovative. We came up with the idea to begin by writing math on the large white board in the pod, so at 7 AM one morning I went and found the biggest math problem I could and wrote it on our white board. As other team members came in they contributed to it and added phrases and other math terms they could find so that the whole board was covered with some manner of "innovative thinking." When people would walk by and ask what we were doing, we'd say things like "this is how we figure out where we are going to lunch." Though it was purely meant as a joke, some months later I was at a company function and after sharing what group I worked with received the response "Oh yeah, you are the guys with math on the board - man you're smart!" Our joke turned into our brand. They associated what we were doing with math and in turn that math was associated with innovation and smarts.

Inside every company are groups working to be innovative that create titles and jobs and appear to develop innovative solutions, but to any discerning eye (in my case, a mathematician), it appears anything but innovative. Too many people sit on the sidelines of their companies with ideas and concepts hoping to gain traction while executives and decision makers are working to keep the lights on in a constant state of survival just keeping up, and unable to focus on the distinct competitive advantages that come from results-driven innovation.

Meanwhile, the technology innovation engine continues to churn out new tools, devices, and systems of tools that create new opportunities for businesses. The challenge is that most of these tools do not fit neatly into simply improving or accelerating the performance of the business that would use them. Rather, they disrupt the structure of organizations, the way products and services are created, the distribution channels, the sales reach, the pricing models, and even the kinds of products and services the business could deliver. Some of the new technologies, while promising, are simply not ready and a business attempting to adapt to them finds this out only after spending a considerable amount of money. Other technologies are used in ways even the inventors did not conceive, and this innovative application makes both the technology and the business user more productive.

There are few roadmaps available to the business leader to pick through the deluge of technology innovation to create a new business model while rejecting those dead-end technologies that would end up being a waste of time and money.

Through interviewing executives, managers and front line employees at companies of all shapes and sizes throughout the US over the past several years, I have uncovered common challenges that companies face when it comes to adopting new technology and creating space for new and potentially disruptive ideas.

"Building the Expo" is the culmination of interviews,

extensive investigation, and time spent with researchers at Carnegie Mellon University and University of California, Berkeley, as well as countless conversations with consultants around the world about the topic of innovation. My two main areas of focus were: what are the success factors in adopting the new technology, and what are the warning signals to determine if a new technology is either not ready or would be a distraction.

My aim is to change the way innovation is used, both in selection and in the adaptation within a business. The challenge comes on both sides of this adoption process. For the technology creator, how the new innovation can be more readily used in the market. And on the business adoption side, what the company will need to do to effectively choose and use the right innovations.

Although there is much content written on the subject of innovation, this book addresses principles discussed in the context of how companies make use of this innovation. It will help companies put real change in motion, along with action steps and aids in effectively using technology to the advantage of the business.

Some businesses, tired of the continual challenges, have fallen into a reactive mode. Rather than trying to be early adopters, they wait on the sidelines, reacting to what others do. This strategy, as Nicolas Carr points out in "IT Doesn't Matter", is only effective in certain circumstances. The big challenge is knowing when to wait, and when to adapt quickly in a global, competitive environment.

This book is not about business as usual. It establishes principles both in business and in other user contexts, on selection, adaptation, and transformation that comes from the use of technology to change the nature of the business.

It is my hope and passion that out of this book, I will also be able to create a community of people around the world that will contribute to the topic of innovation in a whole new way.

In *"The Little Black Book of Innovation"*, Scott Anthony defines innovation as "something different that has impact[1]." If I were to focus on innovation as a topic, I would have a hard time being innovative in that sense. Instead, I will focus on simply making the process of creating things from ideas more effective than corporations do today... After working for the first several dozen companies over the past several years, I began to see patterns appear; regardless of the industry, vertical or city. These patterns showed me how companies take on new factors and how they leverage the word "innovation" in the course of doing business.

You have heard the phrase "necessity is the mother of invention;" if it is to be believed, it is under the most stressful circumstances that the best inventions or more innovative ideas are created. How many musicians have their first album propel them into stardom, only to produce a sophomore album that is less than show worthy? The term "one hit wonder" exists for that very reason. People have their whole life to come out with their first musical album, but then are under the gun in a short period of time to produce a second. I believe the second album flops because the first album had the musician in a place where they were near starving. They put everything they had into their first album working day and night to get their career airborne. Once it has taken off, and they are making real money, there is less stress to make it work the second time around; or at least they are not near starving so there is less pressure to reach the same level of passion as before.

Thomas Edison has been credited with inventing the electric light bulb; however, it was actually an improvement on an invention made 50 years earlier. The concept of the electric light was not new; it simply had not been engineered in a way that was practical for home use. Anyone who studies history can make the argument that nothing is invented from scratch; rather inventions are an improvement built on something that came before it. Some inventions change the tide, such as the iPhone setting a new standard for consumer electronics in enterprise environments. The iPhone itself was an improvement on a class of cellphone that already existed. Apple disrupted that industry by changing the way people thought about smartphones and created a demand unmatched by any consumer electronics brand to date. It takes a certain kind of boldness to step out that far ahead of everyone else and invest time and resources to push past the pack.

Building the Expo is written on the premise that rather than building on foundations companies have in place they try to build something completely new at the risk of revisiting costly mistakes. Do not simply say you are an innovative company; ensure you are producing innovative things that can help recoup the cost of research and development. Too often companies are inundated with people simply talking about innovation without producing anything worthwhile. There have been examples of research and development (R&D) titans that not only managed to produce tangible results from the research they did, but changed the way companies considered how research and development was performed. Take for example, Kelley Johnston and the work he did in developing Lockheed Martin's famed Skunk Works team. The fifteen principles he delivered set the pace for how research is now done at Lockheed Martin. He focused not on what could be invented, but rather what could be improved on in such a way as to produce the most amount of value in the shortest amount of time and to do it in such a disciplined fashion as to consistently create practical outcomes.

The namesake for this book is the World's Fair, or World's Expo. There are often images that jump to mind of the future, concepts of what may come in the next five, ten, fifteen or more years. Whether it is architected buildings utilizing new concepts or kitchens of the future that demonstrate what companies like GE have planned, to transform your home. An exposition is more than just a dim concept and a thrown together display. The work that went into each company's exhibit, displayed for hundreds of thousands to see, was an engineering feat that did not just capture the hearts and minds of the exhibit patrons, but they actually functioned. Buildings showcasing the future did not collapse, kitchens of the future did not catch on fire, and revolving walkways did not maim anyone. There were dioramas, time capsules, and new-aged technology being premiered for the first time. The Expo promised that the world of tomorrow was just around the corner; it inspired hope, and gave people something for which to look forward.

Today, rather than display the future, most companies paint a picture that they are financially sound and that they are continuing to provide the same value, on roughly the same products they had the year prior with minor improvements along the way. New products are unproven and costly, so drastic changes could be an unnecessary risk. Trade shows or the occasional television commercial display may demonstrate some of what this world of tomorrow may look like. To some extent, most companies are considering this "world of tomorrow" and how they can build roadmaps and plans to ensure success long into the future. What happens after the roadmap is not always progress. As any good business person knows, having a cost center is not necessarily a good thing, and though some level of effort is spent regardless of how the current revenue forecast appears, how much time, money, and effort will be spent varies greatly on a number of qualitative and quantitative factors. Google, for example, did not kill "Google Labs" because they were no longer profitable, but possibly as a sign to Wall Street that it is better to be good at a few things than to try and succeed at everything. The 10% rule they were also famous for (allowing employees to spend 10% of their time on side projects or new ideas they had) has been greatly limited, and their R&D division, Google X, is "top secret" and less open about what they are working on.

Imagine a company that is excited to talk about the future, not just behind closed doors or with a certain set of employees, but one that builds products simply for the sake of demonstrating the things we can look forward to in the future. Auto companies are great at creating concept cars, which may never go on sale, for just this reason, but what about insurance companies or gas companies? Although you will occasionally see Chevron discussing some of the smart stuff they are up to, it is rare to see this displayed beyond the occasional ad blip. Imagine a world where everyone was excited to share what they are up to, and not wait until their 100th anniversary (IBM) or a Pro-US jobs campaign (GE) to showcase their plans.

Getting there means being innovative and by following a process that produces results based on a concrete plan which everyone, including your CEO, can get behind.

This process is based on findings from several years working with companies around how they handle and adopt disruption, from cloud computing to mobile devices, and how they do the business of research and development. This book will help to lay out some methods that work for companies today, and begin to lay out a plan for how to take the concept from the expo to the store shelf. Brian Klemmer, a motivational speaker said, "You can either have excuses or you can have results — you cannot have both." Which of these would you rather have at the root of your corporate culture?

Today, around the world, people are sitting in expensive conference rooms full of sticky notes covering every surface discussing the future and coming up with new whiteboard-driven models that will land in a colorful PowerPoint presentation someday in the distant future. It may even end up in a book, TED talk, or an "innovation session," driving millions of dollars in spending and helping create another speaking engagement about the future, which in turn quotes other such activities using the word innovation in the title until it culminates in someone's career doing keynotes for SXSW, and writing 50 page books on thinking outside the box. Years from now, people will look at this massive amount of work, dissect it to see what practical thing resulted from all that innovation, and find it significantly lacking.

The word innovation itself is nearing the point where it is so overused that it is become part of our everyday language when describing one of a hundred different activities associated with ignoring the work at hand and trying to come up with something new for the sake of doing something new. Innovation is a very powerful word when used in the correct context; however, it has become something that involves a lot of time spent talking about ideas that do not ever turn into something resembling progress.

Think of the research and development that happens within your company. Does it result in building the kind of exhibit an "expo" would display that not only works, but leads to stronger company growth as a result? How much time is spent locked in sticky note hell trying to take a concept and get it to take off? Are there politics and overly complicated organizational charts to maneuver to get through the hegemony and onto the results? Even in groups designated as R&D there is more money that gets spent than returned to the point that most companies consider it a necessary evil. More importantly, why does there continue to be dedicated R&D groups when diffused innovation and corporate brain share is becoming the norm? It is a problem every company no doubt experiences, and every employee undoubtedly asks themselves as they see the problems all around them and wonder what the value is in contributing versus setting off and going it alone.

Companies that participated in the 1938 World's Fair could be large and still be innovative at the same time in a way that was both exciting and new. By the end of this book you will have an idea of how to help your company become more innovative — regardless of its size — and help revive the long lost belief that innovation can be forward looking and profitable all at the same time.

When it comes to being innovative, and building a better R&D practice, it is time for companies and individuals to get rid of the stories and excuses and build that expo.

2
BUILDING THE EXPO

When you think about what it takes to make something successful in a company, you will recall stories of great feats where men and women conquered board meetings, inefficient teams, and long drawn out political battles fraught with reorganizations and budget nightmares. Dilbert, Office Space, etc. elaborate on the poorly run corporate culture, and all the various nuances that are all too real for someone that is worked in a corporation for more than a year. Yet, multi-national corporations have the horsepower behind them in terms of influence, capital and ability to shape the average lives of people around the world. Navigating this space to make the biggest influence is not a new topic; it has been discussed in every which way, from organizational effectiveness to six sigma and lean best practices for running a more efficient team. Yet, even with things moving at a rapid fire pace teams can still be plagued by issues that keep them from doing work that is truly moving the bottom line up, and turning the company in a positive direction. Whether its Millennials invading corporate America, or the rise of the mobile device, there will always be something people will get excited about and cast as their savior to bring them to the type of dynamic and exciting atmosphere that most corporate employees only dream of.

Start-ups very much represent a casual, 'come as you

are,' 'work hard and play in the same space' mentality. Yet these companies eventually go public, the founders depart and MBAs come in to build stronger growth for stakeholders. The slinky Fridays and free milkshake bar goes away to be replaced by finely organized filing systems and cubicle walls. The revolutionary idea turns to the battery that fuels the stocks and bonds, which run the modern day economic engine. It may sound like I'm being overly harsh on the enterprise, but there was a time before cubicle walls and neatly stacked filing systems where innovative companies created great inventions and dreamed of a future that was far better than the one they were in.

I am going to use an allegorical example below that many can relate to, at least in part, especially those that have worked in a corporate setting before.

Mack, an engineer, has been tasked by his director with the job of building an innovative product for the company's "kitchen of the future" exhibit at the World's Fair in New York. The theme for the fair was, "the world of tomorrow" so it needed to be futuristic. The challenge about this concept was that not only did the kitchen have to display cutting edge elements and futuristic designs, but it must also function just like a real kitchen. This would require not only an ample amount of time being invested in understanding what was out there and creating a futuristic dream that would help promote the forward looking view of the company, but also leave enough time to build a product that could be packaged and sent to manufacturing for actual production. After being handed his budget and deadline, Mack and his team of engineers went to work on stepping through the processes to understand, deploy, test, prototype, release, and monitor all aspects of the project. He knew they had to develop something unique since the company was committed to attending. They worked within the allotted amount of time with their specific budget and came up with something by the deadline that hit the mark. His department had been working on a number of new concepts for future models of stoves, but Mack felt he should extend the concept to an entire kitchen to fit the Expo's theme.

The first step was to conceptualize the idea in a way that Mack would be able to get the most feedback from his peer groups within the company. He often felt his ideas were shot down not on their merit, but simply due to politics or peer envy. Even though he was normally only in charge of stoves, he was given a handful of broader assignments within this project which affected all of his peer groups. Their buy-in was not critical; however, it was important if he wanted to get the concept off the ground. Mack knew he was stepping into a lion's den because it was a project that dealt with the future. He knew buy-in was critical to receive the funding and support he needed to continue leading his team to move the idea forward into a working model. Based on prior experience, Mack knew this was a project not simply built on a good idea, but also upon a great community effort that would spawn a working prototype that would then help put his company and his own team on the map.

After conceptualizing the idea and gaining the buy-in on the "grand vision," Mack knew he needed to enroll a handful of folks to draft the concept for him in such a way that it provided enough context to serve as an adequate representation of the vision. It needed to be done well enough that he could gain executive buy-in to move the idea forward and get the prototype built. This was something that would require finding people who were willing to work on their own time. This project was a strong focus within the company, but he only had a small amount of hours funded for employees to put toward helping him out. It was critical that he had built up relationships over time that enabled him to gain their buy-off. Even with approval from the higher ups, it was important to get everyone else on board for the project to be fully successful, and then to leverage the buy-off he had to build a prototype, into the additional buy-off he needed to take it into production.

The presentation came down to getting everyone excited about his concept. To enhance the enthusiasm, Mack enrolled the help of his brother, Duncan, who worked in accounting and had a way with showing the numbers of a project on paper and how it could translate into helping one's career move forward. Duncan volunteered off hours to help Mack who had helped him with his career in the past. They worked together and crafted a presentation that showed how buy-in and support of this project at a grassroots level would not only elevate each of the people involved, but also gain them recognition from all areas of the company. After Duncan's presentation, people were engaged enough that they volunteered to support Mack in building up the business case and further refining the ideas to present to their higher-ups. Each of the teams also got together the kind of manpower he needed during the day to build and display this prototype.

Even with everyone's buy-in, Mack knew from experience he would lose a large percentage of the folks because something better would come up, projects would creep into the evenings, and some would just plain forget about the project or change their mind. That left him with a handful of qualified artists, engineers, and a couple of marketing people to help gain the kind of buy-off he needed to elevate the project beyond a token pitch into something that would thoroughly revolutionize the company. The team came together in the evenings and built something truly dynamic and interactive. They even produced a mock prototype by using materials the engineers found to build a scale model of the innovative product they were anticipating.

When the day of the presentation came, Mack brought together each of the department heads along with most of his own team to the boardroom. He went through the product ideas they had pulled together and displayed the prototype kitchen set. Mack had anticipated the considerable amount of 'feedback' and suggestions on things he would need to change. Several questions came up as to why he was spending his time on this, and if it was taking away from other important duties as not everyone had approved of him initially working on this. Mack needed to convince these other leaders to approve of him spending more time and money as the scope of the project grew in complexity and involvement. His own management team had not expected this level of effort, so they were somewhat uncomfortable throughout the entire presentation. Finally, after explaining the potential for the project as well as the size and scope of what he was looking to achieve, the management heads determined to make it a larger project and focused a number of additional resources toward the effort. They decided to hand control of the project over to a more senior leader and gain the approval of the CEO to build an assembly process around the prototype to demonstrate a more hands on approach toward product engineering. Mack was put in charge of his team, but would now need to coordinate with the larger effort this had grown to become. Satisfied that it was at least moving forward, Mack left to debrief his entire team on the outcome, and though their own future involvement in the project was up in the air depending on how this greater team came together, he made sure they get their fair due.

The large project team was then built, and a formal project plan was put in place with a number of executive heads in charge of various aspects. The project was deemed to be more of a marketing effort than an R&D effort. With the potential exposure at the World's Fair in mind, the publicity was the main reason behind the company's efforts toward making this a win. However, given the size of the team and level of effort, the project was considerably delayed. The scope and size changed a number of times as more input was given during the final designs. Manufacturing was also taken into consideration, eliminating many of the original elements Mack had in mind. The plan was refined and constructed to fit a more realistic deadline should the proposed prototype be considered for production, which depended on the level of enthusiasm from the potential customers viewing the display. The production was finally completed, though certain elements were not completed on time, so some non-functional components were substituted to demonstrate potential functionality. The display was arranged, with much fanfare, and Mack ended his role by meeting with his management team and receiving an "atta boy" for a job well done. As he looked back at all the effort he had gone through, and how the project came to fruition, he wondered if there was not a more effective way to complete the engagement.

Companies today, to get things done, must not only deal with internal politicking and legacy infrastructure, but also secure safeguards and best practices to ensure people do not become injured, their company does not get sued, and executives do not step outside legal or ethical lines during the course of business. Red tape and extra heads make it much harder to move ideas and products in a streamlined fashion with little to no friction in an organization. Outside of the organizational issues, internal bureaucracy, and politics we have the added shift in technology with the need to build more efficient systems not bogged down by years of legacy infrastructure. Furthermore, moving '20 somethings' into organizations with large amounts of '60 somethings' that have run the company a certain way for 20 years means there will be a change in the way things are done. Then there are the '40 somethings' managing systems and decisions they may not be ready to fully embrace, either out of cost constraint or their level of comfort. There are many books that deal with most of those issues at a very deep level, along with consultants and university programs that can help with the specifics. True innovation though, can ultimately work in a company despite these issues. The age of the intrapreneur is one where everyone is a small business unto themselves, and can build an internal and external brand for their particular skill set that will set them apart from the majority of people who wait to receive instructions before taking any action.

Risk will be rewarded more often than not, and the drudge of the "way things are done" will give way to a richer and more dynamic way of doing business right up until these innovators band together, create a new corporate culture and eventually fall prey to the same systems they worked so hard against. History repeats itself however, so this should come as no surprise. In the meantime, making the most out of the world you are in means playing by a different set of rules, and not trying to solve every issue but build a reputation for succeeding despite the reasons most people give for falling behind, running over budgets or simply not moving the bar forward within a corporation. Building the expo means building it despite all the pieces fitting together, and learning to define success in a series of small victories and not expecting a grand finale when the process is over and you have changed only a small part of the organization as a result of producing something new and revolutionary. Much like great artists, you may end up not being appreciated until long after you are gone, or be only recognized as having a contribution by the small number of people that see the world the same way you do. Intra-preneurs are not all going to get on the cover of Inc. Magazine, or be lauded as the new business revolutionary of our generation, but they will go home and realize they succeeded where many had failed, and have a successful living as a result of it. The burden of the innovator is that you will see possibility long before anyone else, and only you have the drive and passion to move it forward. At some point you may gain recognition and respect, and have a reputation as someone that can pull it off, but it is a long road with no guarantee of success. If it were a sure thing there would be far less middle management in the world and the GDP for industrialized and educated countries would look differently.

Each company has its own way of "how things get done." The only thing that stays consistent from one company to the next is that each is run by people that do not always have your individual best in mind. You may have executives close to leaving who want to build a name for themselves, or perhaps you do have a director that believes they have your best interest in mind and will kill projects they deem too risky to protect you, and end up putting you in a dead end situation career-wise. With start-ups, the same set of egos can exist in a much smaller space, and one only has to look at the number of start-ups that fail in a year to realize that — despite the size of the company — politics can exist there as well, and though there are many reasons why start-ups fail, politics can play a part. If you're an executive yourself, it may be difficult to determine what's best for your team over what's best for your company. Separating your gut from the hard truths you're faced with is a battle you fight every day. When it comes to evaluating new and risky ideas, the difficulty grows even more so as your own reputation is on the line on behalf of your team. The rock and the hard place you're in make it challenging to gain the right perspective.

It is not just politics alone that get in the way. It can be egos or production delays, perhaps complex geo-political issues, or smaller hiccups that send a critical project awry and will no doubt be blamed because it was innovative and new, rather than having conditions occur that have nothing to do with how new or innovate the initiative is. Dr. Stuart Evans describes the concept of "revision triggers[2]" in his book *"Super-flexibility for Knowledge Enterprises"* as something that occurs in a company that will cause a company to take a position and act accordingly. These "revision triggers" can look many different ways, and either occurs internally or externally, but all too often a company is not prepared to handle them. When the heat is on though, some of the purest forms of innovation make themselves known — much as in the example with the incident on Apollo 13, or during events like tsunamis in Thailand, taking out entire hard drive production facilities — these are great examples of innovative resilience.

Regardless of what circumstances you are in, or what it is you are working to create or change, having a keen focus on making an impact with what it is you are doing by cutting costs or increasing revenue is the goal at the end of the day. Innovation is over-hyped, because it is easier to talk about and much harder to do, and a lot of jobs simply do not require innovation or invention in the mad scientist sense of the word. If you have a job that requires you to do work repetitively, perhaps the improvement lies in simply making what you do quicker, or eliminate it all together. Though you may be worried about eliminating your job entirely, few people that are really committed to being innovative ever have to worry about finding work — they will simply create more opportunities to provide more value wherever they are. As I mentioned previously, being on your own — even when you are on a company team — is tiresome work, and being

DANIEL MAYCOCK

truly innovative and forward thinking is not for every man,
woman or child. Being dedicated to being different may be a
lonely road. It might mean making difficult decisions between
lounging around versus studying areas you have no prior
knowledge of. Or, perhaps, you may be choosing to spend
time working twice as hard at what you currently do to make
it to management rather than going through the pain of trying
to change the organization around you. You get to decide if it
is worth the struggle to convince managers two to three
levels up that you are the most qualified to do something
they have never heard of before, let alone to fund whatever it
is you are looking to do while taking you out of the role you
are currently filling.

Being innovative is not easy, but it is what changes
things for the better. Invention is even harder to do, but can
create even bigger change. I do help outline things you will
inevitably have to do for either option along the way. This is
not a 'ten steps towards a more innovative you,' — it is for
anyone that wants to change what it is they are doing or
seeing in such a way as to make things better and be more
impactful along the way. When a company can have
employees who are all innovative versus having a small
group of people "doing the innovation," it can truly take leaps
forward in both how they compete as well as how they can
positively impact their industry. The key then is not to read
this and become an innovator, but instead, take the
principles or best practices you will read about and
incorporate and share them in what you do so that others will
see the impact and do the same. That is what building the
expo is all about, building something impactful and sharing it
with the world around you, so others can take something
from you and do the same. It is only then do we all start to
become more innovative and become less regressive.

The concept of *Building the Expo* covers the typical
innovation process that you will find in most books written on
the topic these days, but I try and cover less around the
specific steps to being a more innovative you and instead
dive into the areas where I have often seen people in this
line of work trip up. It is not as much about how to execute

on something for example, but what things are required to keep people's interest in the event your team is a handful of bootstrap volunteers doing this work on their own time, or perhaps you are launching a concept that takes several months and keeping people engaged and motivated to get it done on time is a big deal. What I hope you will discover is not necessarily things you have not heard before, but a new way to apply them to your own work, whether you are an executive or low-level grunt, and participate in a dialog with co-workers and both direct reports and higher ups about how effective the innovative best practices you have in place are working. Driving to that result means you are not necessarily building to spec, but it means at the end of the innovative best practice you have a clear outcome and something to show for your work.

3
IF YOU BUILD IT…

In the movie "*Field of Dreams*", Kevin Costner plays a farmer by the name of Ray Kinsella who hears a voice that whispers, "If you build it, he will come," and envisions a baseball diamond. He proceeds to build the diamond, despite the pressures of bankruptcy and financial ruin. He takes a step of faith, and things start to take off for Ray.

One of the characters in the movie, played by James Earl Jones, says this to Ray about people showing up to watch baseball played on his Field of Dreams. "Ray, people will come, Ray. They will come to Iowa for reasons they can't even fathom. They will turn up your driveway not knowing for sure why they are doing it. They will arrive at your door as innocent as children, longing for the past. Of course, we will not mind if you look around, you will say. It is only twenty dollars per person. They will pass over the money without even thinking about it: for it is money they have and peace they lack. And they will walk out to the bleachers; sit in shirtsleeves on a perfect afternoon. They will find they have reserved seats somewhere along one of the baselines, where they sat when they were children and cheered their heroes. And they will watch the game and it will be as if they dipped themselves in magic waters.[7]"

Often when someone sets out to do something unique and different, there is going to be a step of faith to believe it will turn into something spectacular with fellow employees lifting the innovator on their shoulders and carrying them around the office to much fanfare and celebration for the great contribution they've put forward. Much like Ray Kinsella, sometimes you have to build it first and wait for a while, despite all the criticism, to see how the concept comes out in the wash. Eventually, if it is something that finds the right audience, and solves the right kind of problems, people will begin to learn about it and embrace it, to the point they will not remember what life was like without it.

The really disruptive innovations are sleepers at first and sometimes done to great peril of the inventor, with some finding their audience long after the inventor has passed away. If you talk to any passionate inventor though, it is not the fanfare they long for, but the curiosity that must be scratched by continuing to push the envelope and introduce new things to shake up the world around them and make it a better place.

In the enterprise arena, change is not only fraught with the same challenges, but the organization itself has antibodies that are prone to fight drastic change. Simply wanting to bring about disruptive ideas into a large corporation often is not enough and will take a long time, but having a process can help. This process is built on years of experience working with people trying to make changes in their companies and leveraging emerging technologies to make the difference. It is far from comprehensive, and intentionally not written formulaically, because it is a dynamic space. The goal is to develop a starting point and give you a vision of the baseball diamond, as well as putting some frameworks in place so you can take the step of faith with your idea, build the expo, and see who shows up.

This process is based on the steps it would take someone to build an exhibit at a World's Fair and discusses the innovative process from that state of mind. Innovation is such a fuzzy word; it is hard to conceptualize what "being innovative" actually means, despite how many books are written on the topic today. The goal here is leveraging that metaphor to help frame up an approach that weaves together hundreds of best practices based on interviews and first-hand accounts of people in the corporate space doing it correctly, in a way that is easier to conceive than "being innovative."

Conceptualize The Idea:
The Initial Idea

The first step in any concept is coming up with the idea and putting it to paper. Either it is going to come from someone within the company, an idea you came up with, or a project you were assigned to define something new as a solution. Imagine in the context of a World's Fair, you are asked to come up with a new kind of kitchen concept as a marketing tool to get media attention and drive more interest in the brand, but you are only left with past models to build a future vision that will not only display up and coming trends in kitchen hardware, but also not be so far out that it will be years before the product is operational. It often will not be as easy as a vision of a baseball field appearing, so taking your inspiration and your idea a little further and putting a framework around the concept can help to move the concept forward. There is so many things keeping disruption out of most corporations, from the cost to the time to the logistics, that having a clear concept nailed down up front will help to push the first boulder out of the way and get it far well-formed enough to describe to your inner circle.

Draft The Concept:
Preparing the Concept for Your "Inner Circle" of Supporters

Once you have the idea, it is important to keep moving it forward. Once you have crafted a solid concept, it is now time to do the first round of revisions and find both pros and cons of what it is you came up with. Focus on running it by people who are willing to help you by giving real input and able to work with you to improve on your idea before showing it to a new set of stakeholders. Having a method you can use to take the idea and turn it into something real means putting a clear description and definition in place as well as putting it in clear enough terms to get buy-off. This means you can create enough of a picture to get buy-in for funding and support without having to become an expert on all the aspects necessary to create a prototype on your own.

Build The Prototype:
Building the Internal Cut to Get Refined and Work Out the Kinks for Stakeholder Buy-In

A good idea on paper does not always translate to something good in production; even with everyone's buy-in on what it is you are looking to do. Building the prototype means getting the right folks involved early on to build the concept into a form that people can critique and enhance with their insights. You can then refine their input into your dream and head toward the big show.

Refine The Outcome:
Take the Initial Input and Improve on the Concept Prior to Building it

After people have weighed in on what they think of the prototype, how can you make the feedback as meaningful as possible? It is important to make sure everyone's input finds a home, especially that of the stakeholders, without sacrificing aspects that make the concept impactful. There will be a tendency to water the concept down to sustain an existing product or concept already in place, so knowing what to do with the input, while still creating a disruptive vibe with what it is you are doing, is critical.

Execute The Plan:
Prepare the Concept for Display

Once everything has been fine-tuned, it is time to put the concept into primetime. This is not as easy as it sounds though, and there is much to consider in keeping the concept momentum moving even at this stage while making sure that this version of the idea will lead to even more improvements down the road.

Mediate The Dialog
Improve Your Concept From Input Received at the Event for the Next Expo

Once something is in production people will have comments and input that you can use to better refine and grow your ability to push disruptive concepts forward. Mediating the input while you are refining for revisions and gaining insights for future concepts is important to growing your influence, ability and reputation for future initiatives. This can look a lot of different ways, from launching a pilot project online and keeping an eye on social media, to doing an internal pilot and setting up lunches with willing participants to gauge input. People are often not short on opinions, and the more you can involve people in the process of developing something, the broader your eventual audience will be as a result.

Deconstruct The Outcome:
Deconstruct the Concept Once the Event has Passed; Perform a Postmortem

Once the show is over and you are ready to sunset the concept; how will you pull useful lessons away from what you did in preparation for the next concept? Although most innovators are known for the one or two great things they did, there are hundreds of concepts they built and developed besides those ideas that made them truly great. No one concept lives on a pedestal in an innovator's mind since it is history that ultimately decides how impactful it will be. Having a clear plan for taking what you can from the process and building momentum for the next concept is critical.

Repeat The Process:
Turn Your Win Into Something Repeatable

Building a process that spans multiple concepts means

you will be able to take something away from each at-bat and grow a successful career with a concrete reputation. With each win, comes more influence and greater resources to make bigger impacts. Having a framework for a repeatable process means you will go into developing each concept knowing it will lead to the next one, and help establish a growing pattern of successes based on the things you have learned previously.

As I mentioned earlier in the chapter, this process is far from a silver bullet and is not a formula. Rather, it is a series of best practices and frameworks that can help you chisel away at the concrete facade most corporations put up to keep their wheels on the track for the company to continue to stay profitable. Building new concepts into your company and creating a culture of responsible disruption means you will have the benefits of both continued profitability and process improvement, as well as the insight and drive to continue to reinvent the company and help it shift with the times. Companies will change, whether they want to or not, it is just a matter of knowing if it is a change that brings greater growth or puts them on the path to bankruptcy. Each day, that choice is made in various parts of the company and is reflected in public markets, boardrooms and year end reports. However, it is not necessary to abandon the current corporate strategy and become an entirely new company, especially if you are already a profitable one. Building the right best practices in place means you will be able to react when it counts, and be pre-emptive enough to start making the changes before it is a matter of life or death for the company. By helping establish concepts and create disruption inside the company you can help your company take on this manner of thinking and create a more flexible corporate persona that will be ready for the changes taking place today and well into the future.

4
CONCEPTUALIZE THE IDEA

When you think about creating something new, what comes to mind? Is it sitting in a laboratory mixing various chemicals together to create neon green compounds that let off large amounts of steam? Perhaps it is standing in front of a chalkboard wearing a cardigan and drawing up lots of math? For some, it is wearing a black turtleneck, wire rimmed glasses, sitting in red Ikea chairs and drawing various shapes and arrows on notepads while discussing the future of emerging technology. What does it look like for you?

One of my first clients was a company that had existed for a very long time, and was in the process of re-vamping most of their traditional business units to take advantage of new technologies where it made sense. From websites, to data analytics, every large group had a representative or advocate that was interfacing with the innovation team that was a centralized function within the company. Sitting in the first meeting, which was to be a brainstorming session, were folks from many different groups, several from the IT org, as well as a couple folks from the innovation team.

I pulled the project sponsor aside after the meeting and asked why this particular group of people came together for the meeting and if having 14+ people in the room was really productive. It turned out that individuals came, who were interested in the meeting taking place and were therefore allowed to attend and join the team. The project plan and vendor engagement process were simply taken from the way projects and initiatives had worked previously with a focus of including a lot of people up front to gain broad approval. This lead to a lack of real consensus and compromising on the initiatives to get buy off. Furthermore, they were evaluating technologies that changed rapidly, while the decision making process to move an initiative forward would take close to a year.

A good deal of effort was put behind being more innovative, and adopting new solutions, but the company was stuck on the process end which hampered the initiative overall. Even though innovation was at the forefront of the mind, it was difficult to operate in a completely new way, which was necessary to move the concepts forward from a conceptual level.

When thinking about blazing new trails, often the start of those trails comes with a melodramatic moment when the protagonist is hit by inspiration and then feels compelled to start a montage-led scene in which everything else in their life is discarded for the sake of achieving that brilliant epiphany. All too often, the greatest ideas start with an initial idea and take way more time and effort than people expect. There are very few good ideas that simply on paper and potential alone will propel someone to the forefront of thought leadership. In those cases, it is usually because they worked very hard to get to that point, so much so, that on one's heritage genius alone people will take a chance and support an idea simply because it came from that particular individual; regardless of how far along the concept is. Warren Buffet can probably convince a lot of investors to move around their entire investment strategy over a phone call, but it is because he has done the work and built the reputation as a trusted authority on the subject. I doubt he had the same impact right out of school, let alone had access to even call major investors over the phone.

Whether you are at the top of your game, or just getting started, having only an idea often does not get you very far, but it is the important and obvious beginning point. Thinking about what can be done with your idea, rather than forcing a creative idea, is a far better way to process your concept. The world around you will spark brilliant epiphanies as you go through the course of your day. Before you scoff too heavily at the overly simplistic suggestion, consider this story.

I once heard the true story of a woman who, while stuck in traffic one day on her way to her job, noticed that the dots going down the center of the lane were not adhering to the road due to the heat. She thought if she could invent better glue, she would have herself a real winner of an idea. When she arrived at work, which happened to be a chemical plant, she worked with a handful of people in her company to engineer a new type of glue that would keep the dots attached to the roadway. After a number of trials and errors, they were able to create glue that worked well. They then managed to work out a deal with various departments of transportation, and to this day the woman gets one cent for every dot purchased nationwide. Most people would have just been frustrated that they were stuck in traffic, zoned out listening to their radios, or dreaming about a future far beyond the place where they were currently.

Simply looking around and observing things, focusing on what things people need or want, then conceptualizing potential solutions, is the first step to really creating or improving something new. Generally, most people run into hundreds of problems a year and never think, 'How could this be improved upon?' In conceptualizing the idea, being centered and clear headed is always helpful. There are many approaches on how to do this, for instance, take the time to write down things you have observed throughout the day, close the notebook and reflect over it later on in the day. However you choose to focus and reflect on potential ideas, there are mechanisms available to you to better frame an idea in a different way.

During the course of defining what your idea might look like, consider the use case that will be leveraged. What will the business case be? Who would buy such a thing? How would it be used internally? Oftentimes, if your idea sounds bullet proof and ground breaking, it means you have not poked enough holes in it, so be careful if the idea sounds too good. Finding people that can beat up on the idea, point out the obvious drawbacks, and help bring your feet back to solid ground is important. The more you can beat up on it without completely giving up, is important because you will not ask a question or think a thought that someone out there looking at your idea will not think of themselves. The concept does not need to be indestructible to be a good idea, so be sure to gauge for yourself when an idea needs to be dismissed but hold onto the root of the concept because it came from somewhere. Oftentimes, even the greatest inventors go through multiple drafts of their idea before they stumble onto the winner. The difference between a big idea and a bad idea is often how many drafts down the road it goes and whether or not the same root of the idea is focused on. Whether it is the thousands of light bulbs Edison tested before the one worked, or hundreds of banks that were approached before one said yes to funding Starbucks, grit and determination are two valuable tools often neglected, but nearly always necessary to make your ideas move forward. The key with both those examples is that the idea looked a little different each time and even took a slightly different direction each time for both Thomas Edison and Howard Shultz.

In the book, "*Mastery*", George Leonard discusses the definition of mastery. "It resists definition yet can be instantly recognized. It comes in many varieties, yet follows certain unchanging laws. It brings rich rewards, yet is not really a goal or a destination but rather a process, a journey. We call this journey mastery, and tend to assume that it requires a special ticket available only to those born with exceptional abilities. But mastery is not reserved for the super talented or even for those who are fortunate enough to have gotten an early start. It is available to anyone who is willing to get on the path and stay on it; regardless of age, sex, or previous experience.[8]" If we consider ideation in a similar light, we find the same definition can apply. Anyone is capable of coming up with solid ideas, and it can happen in many different ways. The key is to focus on being someone that can think of new things, and over time find the process of thinking of ideas to be a journey, and not a destination. It also means sticking with the idea and mulling it over a number of times, until you have mastered what it is you are thinking about. An immature idea may require you to learn more about areas surrounding the concept and it may require you to do informational interviews with experts, or share it with others more critical of the idea than you might be. While talking to innovative people in various companies, I have been told that during the thinking process they went through based on the initial idea they had, they came up with even better ideas along the way. Perhaps you have a knack for good ideas, but you beat yourself up before it even makes it to paper. Whether it takes millions of dollars to create or several people to get on board, if the idea is a good one; resources are not a concern. Services like Kickstarter exist today to help people without the means make their ideas a reality.

Perhaps it is the hard work you are afraid of, or the "what ifs" that clog your vision. Are you someone prone to stress? Maybe the thought of bringing your idea to light causes anxiety. These are all making you your own worst enemy when it comes to creative problem solving. Having peace of mind and a process to creatively think about your idea is important. Self-esteem, anxiety, depression, doubt and worry are all things that can get in your way and keep you from the excited feelings one gets when coming up with really great ideas. Making a clear goal around how you are going to overcome yourself to even get the idea on paper is step number one, and is what keeps 95% of the world's best ideas from ever seeing the light of day. Often we do more harm to our ideas than anyone else. It is up to each individual to decide if they are passionate enough about the ideas lurking in their mind to risk telling one person and potentially facing rejection or criticism.

Having a system to share that idea is critical, and can hopefully overcome whatever personal barriers are in your way. If it is anxiety or stress, I would suggest taking a yoga class, or learn relaxation and breathing techniques. I can't recommend the best methods for meditation, but I can help you build a plan on how to begin framing up your ideas to prepare to share them with other people.

When thinking of a new idea, it is important to have a way to frame it up so that others can begin to understand and apply the concepts in a way that they can clearly see the benefits of the idea as well. One example is a methodology I use with clients to better explore the application and potential practicalities of the mobile application they are looking to build.

Situation

What is the situation someone would be in to best leverage your idea? Are they on the go and in a hurry or are they relaxing by a pool taking their time? Setting the stage will help create a holistic view of how this idea will be leveraged and help create a better approach towards setting the scene for your idea.

Role

What is the role of the person or persons using this idea? Are they a corporate executive, or are they a homemaker? A person's role will often imply certain things about what they do or do not do during the course of the day, and help you to narrow your focus further than saying, "well everyone could use it." In the example mentioned above, narrowing a role would mean focusing not on all the drivers running over disconnected dots on the freeway, but the role of the DOT worker that has to collect and continually reattach them. Saying something is useful for everyone is too broad a use case to start with, so getting specific on the actual role of the person or persons you think will be impacted the most will help frame up a clearer sense of who it is that will gain the most value from your idea.

Task

What task is the individual performing? If they are in a particular situation and role, you have an idea of their surroundings and the types of tasks they might have to accomplish over the course of a day, but what specifically are they working to achieve?

Interactive Task

Are they performing a task that requires interacting with something? Oftentimes, if the task involves interaction, it means there are dynamic elements at work that will only allow the person to be in certain situations and would preclude certain roles from leveraging your idea. If you are in a dynamic on the go situation, and the interactive task means retrieving data or information for quick input, you probably do not have the role of a tollbooth operator, or city pool lifeguard. Interaction means quick, it means real time, and typically means something that will not take five minutes to complete or require extended periods of focused time; that is what separates interaction from production.

Production-Based Task

Is the task being performed the production of something? If so, situations that require someone to be multitasking or in a dynamic situation typically are not ideal for producing something, which would further exclude certain roles as well. If you are producing a work of fiction, a piece of art, or rocking chair, ideas should support the situation and role that would go with these production based tasks, and hone in on either helping to improve the production of that widget, or increase the number of widgets produced.

Consumption-Based Task

A consumption based task is one where someone is consuming something, whether its food or information. When someone is taking something in, in a way that is not interactive, and providing minimal input or production as a result means someone is taking something in, perhaps to do something with that later or simply consume it out of a passing interest.

Although this may seem like an overly narrow set of definitions to build a scenario for the idea to live, and I could probably list hundreds of additional tasks outside of the three listed, the goal is not to fully develop the idea or concept into something that you could turn around and get funded tomorrow, but rather it is to build enough of a picture of what it is you are thinking to share with someone in an elevator for five minutes.

Mack knew right up front that buy-off meant getting others on board to help him before funding was lined up and executives funded the entirety of his vision. He knew that it would take some persuading up front just to get a handful of his friends and experts in the room to build the polished proposal. He also knew it would take a conversation with his brother, Duncan, to help build the first draft of his concept. Having an idea is great, and brainstorming is also useful, but I do not call out brainstorming early on because the world is full of too many ideas that are not fully thought out. Typically, simply having an idea is not enough to convince anyone else that it is worth backing. Having the simple framework to begin to think through how you will explain it means you will be much more effective when conceptualizing the idea, and getting it to a state that you are ready to share it with others to begin working to draft the concept.

5
DRAFT THE CONCEPT

After getting your idea put together, the next step is to draft the concept and prepare it for presentation. This is often tricky because years of building power point presentations have made the process of drafting and building a concept become very two-dimensional. If you think about why most people watch movies or TV shows, it is to suspend reality for a while and get into whatever story is playing out.

This doesn't necessarily mean you'll need to head out and enroll in a sketching class, or learn 3D drafting, but having a clear way to articulate your concept visually can go a long way in helping you communicate the concept to any sized audience.

Often when I'm speaking to clients, there either isn't a projector in the conference room or there's some technology issue keeping the presentation from being shown. In one particular case, my boss and I walked into a client's office and noticed there was a lot of firefighting memorabilia in the office (they did home insurance). Without the ability to present, we quickly got into a conversation about a relative that fought fires and the client stopped the meeting right there to walk us around the entire building, including kicking people out of the conference rooms to share stories about the material on the walls. At that point, we went from simply talking about our products to connecting on a level that was a lot more meaningful than simply pushing a product. By the time we were finished with the tour we were able to gear our concepts for their business around the things they genuinely cared about rather than the tone-deaf pitch we had prepared. Context is what drafting a concept is all about, because a draft can change, as can the context, but the premise of what you're sharing just adapts as you gain more insight and can build trust in the process.

Drafting the concept doesn't mean creating a drawing, it can simply be a handful of mental bullet points that you can quickly throw onto a white board or describe using a napkin and ballpoint pen; adapt whatever you're sharing to the environment you're in. If you're building a connection with your audience, it doesn't matter the topic, because you'll build the kind of trust that says you have their true interests in mind and from that place you can draft a concept that's tuned into what your audience really cares about.

Chances are good that when you step into the conference room to convince executives to part with their budgets to fund your concept, having them willingly fall in love with the story you are telling will make your presentation more than a diatribe about the company, or a monotone and drab dialog about the future. Create a riveting story based on the situation, role, and task you set up in conceptualizing the idea, and focus around the types of tasks this role carries out today, will carry out in the future, and how their vital support will transport this role into the new century.

Unless you are dealing with a start-up, the thing to keep in mind is that you are not just pitching to get funded when you share an innovative idea; you are attempting to change the fabric of a company. Clayton Christenson, in the book "Innovator's Dilemma", describes two types of companies that compete in the market place today. Start-ups and new entries into the marketplace are more likely to bring about disruptive innovations because larger firms are battling each other to stay relevant. They are focused on sustaining innovations simply to stay in the marketplace they are already competing in. Switching to disruptive innovation when you are an established firm focused on sustaining innovations, does not necessarily make sense right out of the gate. Most established companies, Christenson discusses, will focus on disruptive innovations by investing in small firms focused on those innovations because the older value network is tied to their much more profitable core products where the real market demand and profitability sits. Therefore, larger companies are reluctant to take advantage of disruptive innovations because it could mean anything from competing against their existing technology approach to investing in a first or second round of innovative products that may not gain larger relevance until substantial changes are made to allow for broad adoption.

The reason I discuss this here is that being innovative in an established company can be an uphill battle. Most companies are full of people that would like to think outside the box, but are resigned to punching in every day and only making small incremental improvements to not stand up so tall that their peers try and bring them back down to the status quo. The key then is not to try to change the entire company holistically, or quit in hopes of getting a start-up going that will let you do what you don't think you can do in your present company. It is rather to draft the concept in such a way that will move the needle forward. As your team practices these principles real innovation will grow to other groups in the company because their effectiveness is recognized. Corporations have resources that small businesses do not, so being able to create practical ways to adopt a new disruption in a way that gets funded and sticks means you can buck the trend. This means that for the audience you are presenting to, consider where they are and how much is in their control to get behind and support the concept. The vision should be broad, yet it should also be realistic. If you are in accounting thinking about new ways to build airplanes while working at a textile company, do not expect the vision of new aerodynamic designs to get the support of your senior director.

However, applying your love for aerodynamics into more effective ways to launder textiles, and building the business case around the cost savings means you can arm those closest to the product. They can then, in turn, present it to their superiors and then you can transfer to this new team as the numbers guy on the project, and help those engineers get buy-off to build the pilot. The other option is, of course, getting a job at Boeing, but it is hard enough launching changes in a company, let alone traversing skill limitations and leadership teams with whom you have no credibility. In this case, the audience would not be the executives in charge of funding the aerodynamic shift, but instead selling the engineers at your peer level to move the project forward to their superiors. They are going to be the group that can poke holes in your idea, and it will be up to you to drive the changes forward to gain enough buy-in to move the concept forward. Unfortunately you still have to do your job in the midst of this, any change is difficult and big change is even more so. The key is building the kind of presentation that is adaptable and easy to understand. If it is adjustable, people can take your ideas and run with them.

This will require less of your time explaining it to the next audience. Perhaps you are looking for modest changes instead of something disruptive, or perhaps it is related more closely to something you do for a living. The point is that the concept needs to get to the point as quickly as possible, build the vision that will paint the picture in someone's mind tailored to the audience you're speaking with, and also be something easily duplicated and passed along as you may not always be the one to present it. This sounds easy, right? If it were then you would have probably stopped half way through the first chapter. Though there is not a spectacular 10-step approach toward crafting the perfect message in just the right way, there is a helpful framework that can be used to take the idea from the concept stage into building something meaningful.

Situation: The "As Is" State

This is where you describe the situation today that needs improving. This is the most important aspect of what it is you are drafting because it creates the relationship between the audience and the message you desire to get across. It's also the part of the presentation that, if done correctly, will mean you won't be answering the question, "Remind me, why would we do this?" at the end of the presentation. It is not necessary to depress the audience, but creating a call to action means there will need to be some picture painted to entice people to desire to move forward. Knowing your audience is the most essential here, because you will not sell data points by simply assuming the audience will care. The presentation must be tailored appropriately. You could choose to do informational interviews up front in order to gain a better perspective, or you could also build research focused around your particular group or company in comparison to others in the same industry.

For start-ups it means presenting the ideas to investors by describing the market first, and then the product that is being introduced. Finally, it means creating the stage for which the product will have the most impact. For corporations, it means discussing the situation the employee is in, pulled from what you have developed in conceptualizing the idea, and create compelling enough reasons why something needs to change, so that the audience is drawn into the need for something TO change. More importantly, it should be tailored to something over which the audience has control. If you are discussing the problem with the way tires are built, but work for a legal firm, then it will not matter how right you are; the effect will be limited to your influence, brand, and reputation.

Beginning with situations that you have some level of influence and reputation in, means the credibility of your statements will be more impactful. Even if you work at a company that manufactures tires, start with asking how far you could realistically take this concept if everyone in the room left the meeting fully bought off on the concept. If it's your management team and they love it, how close are they to the situation you described? Your boss may agree over beer that the state of your company is dire, but unless he is tight with the board, broad-sweeping reforms will only gain so much traction. Building the right situation means it is something that will not just resonate with your audience, but propel your concept into reality to get the funding and support you realistically need to impact the situation you're describing, and will come about as a result of the concept in action.

Target: The "To Be" State

This is the part of the concept where you draw on your research to build the business case and describe the realistic and achievable future you are prepping the audience for. This has to be something they can really wrap their minds around and become drawn into with a minimal sense of disbelief, to buy off on the incentive to support you. This needs to not only prove your time so far has been well spent, but that you know enough about what motivates them that you won't miss the mark leading up to the big ask. Grand visions are nice, and make great stories, but it is hard to sell something vague, far out, or overly broad to feel like it is something attainable. You can have a vision for where you want this concept to go, but, as Christensen's research shows, corporations don't buy into disruptive innovation.

There is nothing saying you cannot have a disruption in mind, as well as have a master plan you are working toward, but selling it incrementally and getting some quick wins under your belt will mean building the credibility and reputation to ask for bigger things. Before you discuss targets about reducing the company's entire overhead cost by 10%, prove you can save the team's overhead cost by 1%, then work to leverage the same system in bigger ways over time. Incremental improvements mean you can fail fast, and fail often, without getting the wrong kind of reputation in groups that only know you based on what they hear from other people.

Imagine having a ten step plan to build something grand and revolutionary, but only selling one step at a time. If that one step has enough meat on the bones and what you spend time or money on brings about an improvement, who cares how big it is? Most managers and executives, when presented with a way to save time or earn more money will typically consider it. But, try selling too much, say a hundredfold return, and it will sound too good to be true. Selling a double the return on something is impressive, so if you know you can hit it, start with an offer of a 1.25% return and then over exceed that expectation. However cliché, it's true that you should always under promise and over deliver.

Building the target vision is no different, and a small change done successfully in a well thought out manner will go much further than something entirely mind blowing. Not to say you should stay small, but getting the reputation for pulling off big things takes time and will eventually lead to the ability to bring about disruption over simply sustaining changes to the company, and will give you the kind of reputation equity you need to achieve that grand vision.

Proposal: "Filling The Gap"

When coming down to the ask, it will depend mostly on how you built the situation and target, and how bought-in everyone is. However, you can blow it in the ask no matter how well thought out the previous two points were, so the focus here is to think like an entrepreneur. You have a certain amount of resources and ability to do things based on your role and position in the company. If you are asking for something, it means you need more than you have, and that is going to require someone to have trust in you and your ability to deliver.

The first time out of the gate, you are a poor college graduate with no proven track record asking an investor to take a gamble on your brilliant business idea. This investor does not want to give you a salary and pay your way, they want to see you be motivated and hungry, putting everything on the line, so you will produce a return. For that reason, they might give you less than you need, or only fund you for a short period of time, to keep you hungry enough to get them a return.

An executive is going to think in a similar fashion by

giving you a short runway but you are going to have to be diligent and work to demonstrate not only that your concept is solid, but that you have what it takes to deliver. It may mean working on the weekends to hit critical deadlines, or putting things on the line that make you a bit nervous. Having your job on the line is the extreme scenario and usually only matters if the executive has something to gain from you no longer working for them, after all, collateral only counts if they gain something of value if you don't come through. As most prudent executives and investors hedge bets however, they won't let your first concept extend them past the point of no return and this gets into the scarce resource allocation. As I mentioned earlier, this space is not for the weak and is hard work, even more so when it is within a culture not prone to drastic changes. Therefore, be prepared to comprise on what you need to get the job done, and always have an answer for how this work relates to your job. For that matter, your job will most likely suffer as a result of you charging down this path.

In Mack's story, he was tasked by his manager to execute on the concept for the World's Fair, and had permission to spend some time on it. In the information above, it may sound like I changed the story and started discussing how to talk people into something you might not have permission to do, and to step outside of your role to accomplish it. That is not the case, however, because the end of Mack's story concludes with his "charter" moving out of his control to a larger team effort, with a small incremental change and too many people involved in the end result.

Even if it is your job to be innovative and think about new things, chances are that your most innovative and ground breaking ideas will not end up looking the same way they began because corporations are large and complex engines that have a tendency to shift and change concepts before they are spit out as the final product. This is not always a bad thing, as any publicly traded company has to balance risk with return, but it is also what proves Christensen's research, that start-ups are more likely to create the really big ideas, with larger companies only picking up the torch as a "me too" survival technique.

Big change in corporations is possible, and being disruptive can bear great fruit in any corporate setting, but it needs to be done in just the right way. The way you construct the concept and gain the initial buy-off will set you up for this kind of success and help drive the culture to shift as a result. It is not about having a department of innovators all creating things in a small box, while the rest of the company lunges slowly forward into obscurity, but rather it is about building a corporate culture that can be disruptive and flexible while being able to withstand corporate constraints and external revision triggers.

Even the most enthusiastic and supportive executive needs to perform appropriately, and has their own set of constraints and targets to keep in mind. Being shot down and told your concept is not appropriate, realistic, or feasible does not mean it is without merit. Oftentimes, sponsors or investors have considerations they're thinking about before the meeting starts. Understanding as much as you can about where they are coming from will give you a better sense of what they are able to do prior to sitting down for the big ask. Due diligence and relationship building can go a long way in getting a better sense of how far you can stretch the first step, and making sure it will stay contained enough to drive toward your ultimate goal.

Had Mack kept the idea to himself long enough to produce the result he was looking for, and only pitched enough of the concept to get a small prototype out of the gate before pitching the bigger goal outside of his team for a World's Fair expo, could he have had more control over it?

Looking impressive and becoming promoted means you are leading the department, instead of relying on the good nature of higher ups you haven't met prior to the meeting. This means you will maintain more control within the bounds you are able to control, and leverage the people reporting to you in a way that will incrementally deliver results and gain more and more ground for you to work with.

Although it begins with a well-drafted concept, how you present it matters even more. Dress in a way that reflects responsibility, and remember that how you show up will help people determine how much they can trust their money and resources with you. Dressing in jeans and a t-shirt says casual and relaxed. Would you invest in someone that was casual and relaxed, or would you want someone that takes his or her job seriously, to drive something new and innovative forward? I am not saying you have to splurge for a $6,000 suit, especially when you are presenting yourself as someone with no money, but be aware of how your attire and attitude comes across, and whether or not what you are asking them to take a risk on is adequately met with the preparation and impression you are going to leave behind for them to make that decision on. Most start-ups are not bought just for their product or patents, but also for the people. The world is full of good ideas, but is limited in people that have the ability to create something from nothing, and the drive to bring things to successful and profitable conclusions.

6
BUILD THE PROTOTYPE

You have made the big pitch, and pulled the resources together to move the concept forward into a prototype. This may be your first pitch off the mound, or perhaps you have had your idea shot down a handful of times before you got here. Investors I have talked to in the past will say that they would rather back someone that has failed at least once and has gotten back up, because it gives one some of the greatest life lessons along the way. Failure to gain buy-off the first time is not a bad thing, and most people will have a tricky time getting any level of buy-off without a strong track record, but the sooner you are open to the possibility of failing, the sooner you will figure out how to succeed and have a clear track record for persistence and commitment toward your vision. However, you must be open minded in considering the difference between a bad presentation and a bad idea. No one wants to be the rock star that was never signed to a label, and won't give up the band because they think it is just a matter of time rather than admitting they simply do not have the musicianship to excel. Do you want to be an accountant crafting ideas for new types of airplanes? You may present it a million times, but it could also mean you need to head back to school and get more fundamentals down on aerospace engineering before you are taken seriously. This is just as true in building the prototype as it is in building the presentation and gaining buy-off.

Chances are good you would not have made it this far if those that invested in your concept and gave you the resources you needed, didn't believe in your ability to pull it off successfully. As I mentioned earlier, you have had your whole life to come out with your freshman album, but your sophomore album means the difference between a one hit wonder and a legendary performance artist. Now that you have given your presentation, and the project is a go, you are no longer in obscurity with the corporate hierarchy; you have a name and somewhat of a reputation or impression to maintain in the eyes of people that can determine your future in the company and potentially elsewhere. It is now time to deliver on what you said and come through in a successful way. Your presentation was the freshman release, and you got a hit, now it's time to come through on the sophomore hit and show you are not only good at presenting, you are even better at delivering.

When you think about the team you are going to build to help be successful in this space, some of them will be directly reporting to you at this stage of the game or they could be dotted line resources that have a part time obligation to support you. Some others need to be coaxed and prodded to jump in and help because they are the best at what they do. Regardless of how the resource plan for the prototype goes, there are universal rules that apply to building a team and certain things to keep in mind when determining whom the best fit would be in the organization.

A couple of things a typical Project Manager would tell you might be things like — developers need to not go more than three months without a deadline, or having everyone perform a personality profile can help alleviate hidden land mines along the way so you can pair compatible personalities together. I am not an expert when it comes to organizational effectiveness, as areas like change management have their own sets of professionals, but I will offer up a framework that was taken from "Super-flexibility for Knowledge Enterprises" which can help put teaming in a better state of mind.

The Clustering Dimension:
The Anatomy of the Organization

How your corporation is built from a hierarchy or management perspective will affect a majority of the decisions that are made in the organization. More importantly, it will determine how likely you are to influence various parts of the organization, and how you will partner with stakeholders in groups potentially beyond the scope of your prototype in order to get a holistic enough team together to get the job done. If you work in the engineering group, and marketing is contained as part of the same organization with only a few executives to chat with to get a marketing resource, branding as part of the prototype roll out will be far easier to maneuver than if the marketing team is in another division of the company, with an entirely different request system. Knowing whether or not you do chargebacks for requesting labor, or can simply leverage shoulder taps to get quick jobs done, will be a critical component in considering how the team will be assembled.

Having a clear understanding of the anatomy of your company will also help in understanding the potential impact of what you are working to achieve and how broad of an impact it will have based on how many levels of leadership it is required to pass through. If you are a low level manager on the overhead side of the organization, trying to impact the production side of the company will be very difficult due to your role and expertise viewed through the eyes of someone that sees your organization as a cost center versus a revenue generating function. This gets back into the type of impact you are looking to make, working toward a quick win rather than something that will become overly complicated and delay progress due to the internal politics of your organization. Those politics are most clearly visible by how the anatomy of the organization is structured more often than not. It is best to avoid striking up conversations around your project in groups that have no connection to you or your efforts. Leveraging resources you have some level of influence with, or that can easily be obtained through a formal request or help desk ticket versus sending e-mails throughout the organization will go a long way in helping you deliver. This can also play a big part in how much of a person's time you are looking to obtain as the anatomy of the organization can inform you on whether someone is solid line, dotted line, or task-by-request, and how that will impact the overall success of your project. Listing resource constraints as a risk early on means the conversations can be mitigated and maneuvered through much more easily than when you are nearing the deadline and are then in a mad scramble to get resources for whatever outlying tasks are left to complete.

The Connective Dimension:
The Circulation of the Organization

How decisions are made does depend on the anatomy of the organization, but what also matters is how those decisions are circulated. Is e-mail the go-to standard for sending in requests? Does each request need to be filed in a particular fashion? What kind of paper trail is required when filing a formal request? Is shoulder tapping okay in certain circumstances, or should everyone's manager be CC'd on e-mails regarding how they will support your task? Having a clear sense of how requests are circulated is critical to knowing what kind of response you will likely receive. Yes, everyone can e-mail the CEO of a corporation typically, but why would you? Having a reason behind the method you use can go a long way in getting the correct kind of responses, and making sure your prototype can be assembled in a way that doesn't spin up too many destructive threads. It is a sad reality that people will intentionally sabotage a project either because they were not included, they don't feel it is important, or simply have no intention of helping someone without there being something in it for themselves. Even the most efficient organizations have people with too much time on their hands, such is the nature of any company over a certain headcount, and this can muck up the gears as much as it can help expedite requests and move the ball forward. Corporate gatekeepers are important to befriend, and never underestimate the power of an office assistant or chief of staff when it comes to meeting with an executive.

The Cohesive Dimension:
The Personality of the Organization

The most important aspect and least understood, is the personality or cohesive dimension of a company. It is often through talking to someone that has worked there for a number of years or a company recruiter whose job it is to profile the employees so that you gain an understanding of what the core personality is. A company is made up like Frankenstein's monster, with parts of branding and internal marketing combined with employee retention exercises and time spent working in different parts of the company. Just as cities, or neighborhoods each have their own distinct personality and reputation, so do divisions and entire companies. You would not expect a product such as an airplane to go through drastic and unproven changes, so why would you expect Boeing to be a radical and highly dynamic company? Yet, Boeing can build a 777 airplane in their Everett, WA factory in three days. It is not because they are highly dynamic and fast moving, but rather they have worked hard to perfect and streamline their manufacturing process. There are many companies, from AT&T to eBay, regardless of their product, that are large publicly traded enterprises and as such, do not change as rapidly as they sometimes need to.

The personality of the company can often shape the perception internal employees have, regardless of how large they are. If employees believe changes take forever in a company, no one will feel the need to rush things through the pipeline. If the company is known to keep 'dead weight' around beyond the point they are useful, expect a lot of high performers to leave in short periods of time with that very same 'dead weight' sticking around to run things. Knowing the personality creates a realistic view of what you can expect outside of the group you have direct control over, and even then, will influence potential outcomes. Motivating employees to do good work isn't always enough sometimes, for instance, if your company sells insurance and the prototype is going to affect actuarial tables and rates for insurance products traditionally sold, delivered and maintained in a certain fashion to produce a certain profit to loss ratio. As I mentioned earlier, it doesn't mean you should give up changing and working to fix the status quo, especially if the personality of the company is causing low performance overall, but be prepared to navigate through this and consider how the personalities of various groups might add to or take away from your efforts to build the prototype.

In keeping these three aspects in mind, you will have a better sense of how your organization works today and how you will navigate through it to get the resources you need for success. However, building the right team in and of itself is not enough, unless you have the right process to actually build the prototype itself. If you have spent any time in software development over the past several years, then you are probably aware of Waterfall and Agile development methodologies. I won't go into Waterfall, but it is important to have a working sense of what Agile is, not to become an agile master, but rather to keep the principles of iterative releases in mind as a way to build a minimal viable product.

This is important, because it is the simplest thing you can construct that will be considered an actual product, which is the crux of this entire book. Too often, "innovations" are simply improvements on something that is already a product, and this sustainment means you are getting the biggest bang for your buck, but it may not necessarily upset large parts of your industry. A minimally viable product, however, means your prototype actually does something useful by the time it is finished, and could be considered something palatable in the eyes of stakeholders and customers. Agile is helpful in the software world, because it sets up iterations that, when completed, can be considered a minimal viable product for the software being developed. It is a milestone in which you can consider a certain aspect of the overall work completed, and the "module" is then stored as part of the overall project with the next sprint attacking the next aspect of the software program. Perhaps your project is a piece of front end functionality, maybe it's doing the graphics for the buttons, or it could be building a part of the backend out for connecting to a data source. The point is, at the end of the sprint, it is something different and usable.

In thinking about your prototype, whether it is something physical or perhaps even digital, do you have the expertise to know how to break your prototype apart into phases so you can start with something you are able to add to along the way? Let's say your project gets cut short, and you only complete a portion of the project. What are you left with? Do the pieces you built have any reusable quality to them? Or are there aspects of the prototype only useful as it relates to the project in and of itself? As large-scale projects are assembled, this kind of thinking is second nature, just like building the oven doors separately from burners and enclosures before the final stage that produces the complete stove.

Basic supply chain logistics will take into consideration where it is most cost effective to do each part of the assembly before bringing it all together. Perhaps there are groups assigned to different parts of the product, to where you would need to bring in hundreds of people to correctly develop and construct a new oven given how disparate and separated each of the aspects of the product are. This can be daunting to think about, and even more challenging to build the system for. Given the task at hand however, if you are working on an oven of the future for this expo, much like Mack was, having product and project managers on your team with the ability to handle logistics is essential, but more importantly, it requires thinking about how the product itself can be produced in phases and stages in such a way that if after a week everything was scrapped, what is already produced could still be useful. This might mean more documentation along the way, it could mean going back a second time before one aspect is considered complete to make sure there is some level of description so a layman elsewhere in your company could someday make sense of it, or it could mean commenting your code even though you think it's excessive and unnecessary. Reuse is something companies today fundamentally lack simply because these steps are not taken in most aspects of the business.

Although executives and decision makers may enforce some level of reusability, many half-done efforts are scrapped. We could debate whether this is due to lenient inventory controls, product management discipline, or any number of things; however the point is that beginning to incorporate reuse and breaking things down into minimal viable components is one way to effectively seed disruptive and radical change in your company. Creating building blocks others can use, developing platforms to make it easier to repeat what you did, or having documentation on what you did readily available means that every module or stage you performed will have some usefulness beyond the project itself.

Revision triggers can come from many directions, and we cannot anticipate the majority of them. Having a project charter and job to move forward and create new prototypes does not guarantee an earthquake will not occur in a production facility somewhere in the world with the ramification meaning everything you were working on is immediately cut, effective immediately. Life happens, and things are out of your control often, but this is another way in which shaping change and building innovative and disruptive things in your company begins. It is about being flexible with what comes at you, much like a start-up who sees their product patents challenged in court, or a hostile takeover threatening the production of a new line of products can jeopardize a bigger vision for shaping the industry.

Chances are good that if you got the charter or the permission, you know the fundamentals of how to move forward and produce a valid prototype. If not, then I would suggest going back to your proposal and getting whatever formal or informal training you need to take this on. However, just because you have the knowledge on how to build it doesn't mean you have the correct approach in mind to make a lasting and disruptive impact in your organization or company beyond the project you are attempting. The point of this chapter is to point these considerations out as even the most seasoned practitioner can get lost in the weeds and lose any ability they once had to radically shape the outcome of projects within their company and industry. Taking a moment to lift your head above the dust cloud, and keep your perspective on what you are building, and how useful it is beyond just doing the task, will mean your prototype will have a greater impact than the sum of its parts, as well as give you the reputation of someone who produces more value than they leverage. This gives you the leeway to slowly take on bigger and bolder things, which is what the goal of building the expo is, after all. However, once it is built and you're off to the races, how do you refine what you have and focus on continual improvement? It is not enough to build once and walk away — leverage what you have built to build something better and take away lessons from that which was accomplished and you can build a singular task into a dynamic and influential track record.

7
REFINE THE OUTCOME

At the point the prototype has been constructed and is ready to be presented you should be thinking about getting a wave of feedback coming in from stakeholders and peers alike.

Some time ago, there was a new product launched, which was code-named Ginger and created by the well-respected inventor Dean Kamen. Information leaked several months before Ginger's release, with notable innovators such as Jeff Bezos rumored to be involved. The press stipulated about everything from heralding the future of automobiles to the future of transportation itself. When the product finally launched, everyone quickly discovered the Segway was simply a terribly expensive scooter that today is selling primarily to tour groups and local police forces and not really revolutionizing the way we experience transportation. It's always hard to predict just how much success a product will have before it goes public. There's no place more crucial to bring in your harshest critics as when you're looking to refine the outcome of your prototype before taking it on a road show. Too often we surround ourselves with supportive people that always have our back, but can leave us blindsided by the real response the broader world will have in store once the prototype goes public.

In thinking about how a garage inventor gets off the

ground, they first build the prototype then slowly seek larger waves of people to review their product and validate its usefulness before the big reveal, at which point it is a make or break event in the world at large. In an enterprise however, boom or bust can happen as soon as you show the overly social workmate what you are up to, or present it to the wrong group of stakeholders before you're ready for a larger roll out, so getting the kinks and downsides ironed out of the concept before going primetime is even more critical. If we consider how this works in terms of biology, all you have to compare is a new human compared to a new horse, puppy, giraffe, etc. Stay with me here — when a new child is born, how long before it can walk and fend for itself? How about a horse? Shortly after a horse is born, as is the case with most animals that grow up in the wild, they learn to walk and eat on their own pretty quickly because they don't have the time to spend years on developing those skills.

It is out of survival that this is the case, because human babies are not living in the wild and are much more complicated when it comes to development, and also are not in the situation of having to stay mobile and avoid predators like an animal born in the wild might have to. When you start talking about what you are working on, it gives the impression that it is something to bring up around water coolers or happy hours. Once you have built the prototype and have begun to show it to people, it had better be able to walk and feed itself, or predators will find it first. This gets back into the previous chapter somewhat, in that an overly complicated or overly disruptive concept will get hampered along the way unless it's released in phases that are easily contained and useful in and of themselves. A dog is not as complicated as a human, but when it's born it is much more self-sufficient initially and will mature faster, however it comes at the cost of a shorter lifespan and less function in the grand scheme of things.

When it comes to your first bold concept, it is about survival, not about lifespan and functionality. If it can walk on its own right out of the gate, then it is easier to defend than if you must wait for it to slowly mature. This is not to say that it cannot evolve over time as more aspects are added to the concept while it works through development, but having a minimally viable product means it does something useful the first time someone has a chance to interact with it.

This then, gets into how to premier your "first draft" to stakeholders and peers, and refines the outcome to build a better Version 2. The first step is determining whose input is helpful, whose input you need, and whose approval is routine or who needs to sign off on it out of regulatory compliance. With each of these three groups, it is important to practice a sales method, deemed "For or against." If you think about selling a car, for example to a married couple, the points you will bring up are either for something or against something of importance to them. Knowing the husband is into sound, you will want to talk about things in favor of this particular car; the for statement being something like, "I can tell you're into premium sound, this car has it," since he's for big sound. The wife, on the other hand, is worried about safety because they have two kids. Discussing safety features in a manner like, "I know you're concerned about safety, and even though this car has premium sound, it's not a sports car and is quite safe." This is important because she's against being unsafe, and premium sound is often associated with an unsafe vehicle.

As it relates to your concept, consider statements that support profitability and cost reduction, as things the individuals will be for. You can also discuss how this is lightweight and fairly affordable, since executives are against wasteful spending. Phrasing your points in terms of for or against will mean that you will be able to speak to people that are all for innovation and change, but also make sure to include rational cost saving comments for those AGAINST innovation as an empty buzz word and a less than useful endeavor.

The People Whose Input Is Helpful

This is the first group to whom you will need to demonstrate the prototype, and should be made up of people whose opinion you trust and can help you see flaws you missed as you are heads down in the work. If it is a team that helped construct the prototype, having everyone review everyone else's work as part of the overall construction of the prototype can be a great way to build cohesive teaming. If it's something you constructed on your own, then perhaps find peers or friendly managers that can weigh in on what you have built, but are able to keep it to themselves until it is ready to be deployed. A lot of start-ups will go into stealth mode as the product is being developed, then slowly open it to beta testers and investors under extensive Non-Disclosure Agreements (NDAs) to refine and improve until it is time to launch the product. Fight the urge to tell more people than you need to, as it's better to see the finished product than hear about it. Getting caught up in your passion can be dangerous, because too many people hearing about something you are working on before you have anything to show might cause stakeholders to get antsy and cause you to prematurely release the prototype into the wild.

The People Whose Input You Need

This should be the group you visit next as you will want the least amount of friction when it comes to gaining their buy-off but don't want them to be the last group in line in case they hear through the grapevine that you have been out and about showing something off. They need to be able to weigh in on it themselves. This group will typically consist of stakeholders, sponsors, and managers whose blessing and faith you earned in first presenting the concept to move forward. Having a clear sense of the value proposition, taken from the presentation during the original proposal, will help inform you on how to present what you have come up with. Whether you are in a small, medium, or large size business, a clear value proposition stated as the prologue to your presentation will go a long way in pulling the bullets out of an antagonist's gun, and help you focus on how to improve rather than to prove the concept you're putting on display.

The other important thing to do here is to always take notes and pay attention to what they say; even if you do not think that what they are saying is useful. Regardless of the feedback, people's buy in matters regardless of how much of it is incorporated down the road. The smallest detail in their mind may be the one thing they look for in Version 2. When it comes to Version 2 and beyond, incorporating their feedback into the next presentation will go a long way to gain their approval, as most people want to be heard and truly appreciate when what they have voiced is acknowledged and incorporated.

The People Who Need To Sign Off

The last group would be made up of any groups that need to approve the prototype due to compliance or regulatory reasons. It may be people that think they need to sign off on something and don't, or could be someone that doesn't think they need to sign off on it but do. Know who these people are, find out what steps need to be taken, and state to your stakeholders early on if the black box that these requests will head into will delay the project's deadline. Security is often on the list if it is dealing with applications or software, and depending on the company policies, can take an extraordinary amount of time without executive shoulder nudging to move it up the list. Regardless of what holds the project up, it's your project, so making sure your project management is transparent on any potential bottlenecks is important. Go by the book, and do not use shoulder tapping or pulling strings because taking shortcuts when it comes to regulations, security, finance, legal, etc. is a quick way to get in deep water.

After getting the support you need, it is time to head back to the drawing board and evaluate how to refine what you have into something more palatable. Regardless of how many prototypes you end up building before declaring the concept ready for execution, each time you head out to review the next version, remember, more will be expected but perfection is never the aim. Buy-off means it is good enough, as you are aware by now that this, even in its final form, may be one step of many to achieve the disruption you are aiming for down the road. The prototype is a step towards the final product, but the final product may represent one piece of the larger picture. Regardless of whether or not a step comes after finishing this concept for you, achieving mastery in something is a process and not a destination, according to George Leonard in his book "*Mastery*". The lesson you want to keep from feedback is not how close to perfect your concept is, but what you yourself get from the process as you begin to work on the new revision. Good enough does not mean settling, it means getting to that viable product that will produce value with the knowledge that you will have to do this many more times before you get close to mastering any aspect of what you have done. This will test you, and show if you have the drive and passion to continue on down this path or leave it where it lands and move onto something else. If you are building a software application, how passionate are you about being a developer? If you are building a new kind of wing, how interested are you in aerodynamics? If you are an accountant working on a kind of jet propulsion, how much can you focus on improving if it is a side project or part time job for you?

These questions may come up in the process of taking in feedback, so be prepared for the external and internal barrage you will get hit with, and remember no one will typically be as negative as you are with yourself. It is not honest unless it is coming from multiple sources, so if you are the only one downgrading yourself, it's time to listen to other voices, not just your own. On the other hand, if you are the only one that thinks going down the path you are headed toward is a good one, then you don't really trust the people whom you have selected to get helpful input from. The key to gaining validation along the way is to filter out bad ideas from the good ones and to be able to recalibrate the thought process and production path you are headed down in a setting you deem safe. As long as you call what you are working on a prototype, the expectation level will be different than releasing a child into the wild and experiencing a disaster. Even Version 1 of a product is still considered somewhat of a trial. Many conservative pockets of consumers will hold off until Versions 2 or 3 come out, waiting for the bugs to be worked out. This is what makes disruption so difficult because it is painful and expensive to gain mass adoption of any product. Once you are there, it is a temptation to slightly modify what is already proven as a winner.

Although there is no one method to vetting feedback, here is a helpful framework that might aid in your thinking on how to revise what you have to get it to a place where it is ready to hit the broader marketplace.

Why Does This Need To Exist?

You should already have a pretty solid answer at this point as you have built the business case and stated the target. If you haven't, then you have gotten far without a clear plan around what the need is in the first place. Perhaps the stakeholders you presented to were lenient because they were placating you, or perhaps they didn't think it would get this far. At this point, you are leaving the theoretical behind, and stepping into the real dollars and cents of moving your concept into something that will be produced and sold. Even if you think you have nailed this, go back and see if something has changed, and make sure you have not missed anything along the way. Get feedback from end users or stakeholders, this may influence the "Why" before it comes time to presenting the final cut and getting the kind of buy-off you would need to move this into reality.

How Will It Meet Demand?

This is more complicated to answer than the first question, but should be asked at some point along the way when considering what would have to change in the company's existing capability to produce and meet demand for the concept as it rolls into production. Having at least a vague notion of what the implications would be for this concept will go a long way to pull more bullets out of people's guns and help move the theoretical into the practical on your own terms. Not having an answer could cause the plan to be easily dismissed because of a perceived difficulty. Not that everyone should be a supply chain expert, but having conversations or reading up on the existing cost of goods sold at your company might give you a more realistic grasp of what it would ultimately take to do what you are suggesting. Even if you are not the expert, you can find experts at various levels of most companies who are easy to access given the right amount of friendly motivation.

When Will We See A Profit?

This question will come up multiple times when discussing the investment and what the financials look like in regards to cost/benefit, return on investment, and total cost of ownership. If you are just working to change or improve something already in place, or perhaps roll out a concept that is not a product, it will not be as bad. Regardless of what you are aiming to accomplish with your concept, be sure to have some sense of what it will cost in the long run, and what it will earn or save.

How Much Will It Cost To Produce?

Whether or not the product will be launched to customers or built and deployed internally, having an overall sense of the cost to deploy is just as important as knowing how profitable the concept will be once it is in production. Knowing the ins and outs of what something will cost may exceed your ability or job code, but if you are building something in a company that is at least somewhat similar to something already being built, then there is probably a good chance someone has an idea of the overall cost of production. If not, there are people who are pretty good at estimating a project, so consider getting to know someone with those skills in order to get a clear picture of the overall cost of production. It may be ballpark figures, but removing the bullets from the guns of those who might want to shoot your project down means you are anticipating questions like this, especially if they are against the project and believe you won't know the answer. The unfortunate thing is that you might not even be in the room when someone brings up the question, so giving a good stab at overall impacts of the business focused around cost is something that is important to circulate well and often.

What Is This Based On, Or Similar To?

To really be disruptive and shake up the foundations of a company is very difficult, if not almost impossible in most cases. Often, it is easier to leave a company and create a disruption that causes the company you left to react defensively and try to buy you or compete with you in a desperate act of survival. Therefore, starting from scratch and developing something with no ties to anything that is already in place is not a good idea when it comes to trying to make effective change in an enterprise take off.

At a previous company, I took 30 years of academic research and applied it to a traditional process to show how incorporating new technology into an existing process, in this case mobile technology, can save millions of dollars. I knew it would not take off in that particular situation or do too much to disrupt things, but I did know it would send a ripple effect throughout the company to consider how mobile technology could impact every aspect of the workplace. This project was used as a martyr, in a sense, to help inspire others to consider the same benefits for their particular role. Three years after leaving, I found out that the work I did served as that very tool to help educate and "crack the ice" so that melting began to occur as mobile became more globally accepted and embraced. Was mobile disruptive? At the time, it was very much so. Was I ahead of my time? Perhaps, but the project was not designed to save millions of dollars, it was to demonstrate that mobile could save millions of dollars. It was based on 30 years of academic research from Carnegie Mellon University and Berkley University, so I was not coming in with ideas from my own little bubble. In addition, it was grounded in my master's thesis, so I had a solid reason to be doing the work in the first place. Furthermore, I documented everything I did in a way that was usable and applicable to different business units within the company because I knew this would be a battle I would never win, but the propaganda coming out would be far more useful in a pen versus sword parallel.

Leaving that company, I took those academic principles applied there and have been developing strategies using those same methodologies ever since. To date, seventeen Fortune 500 companies have used those principles. I have spoken with over 950 executives about the work I did at my previous company, and have shown them how building a new concept based on years of research from an existing topic is the ideal to build upon. Because I could answer the question, "Where have you done this before?" the work had a far more palatable impact than if I walked into the company spouting that I had the silver bullet to fix everything in the company with nothing to base that statement on.

Having a clear sense of what foundation you are building your concept on, and that you are only slightly improving something that is already out there or taking two unrelated things and putting them together means you will have a much better shot at refining the outcome and getting a clear value proposition in a way that people think you can actually pull it off. Being disruptive and innovative is still possible of course, but it is easier to say you are building an electric version of the gasoline lamp, than it is to describe the impact and potential for light bulbs before anyone has seen one. Having your concept grounded in something people are at least somewhat familiar with, means it will be palatable and easier to swallow when it comes time to ask for funding.

It is one thing to build a prototype, and entirely another to move something into production. Although you may not be a supply chain logistics guru, having at least a fundamental understanding of the questions above will give you a foot up against most concepts thrown at product teams from various parts of the company, and will go a long way in demonstrating that this is not a flash in the pan but something you have put thought and consideration into. For some, it may launch them into a new career because they impressed the people they presented the prototype to. For others, it might mean permission to spend more time, or all their time on refining what it is they created, to move it into something even more tangible. Regardless of your intention in putting effort behind this in the first place, once you have buy-off and plan on moving forward it's time to discuss what executing the plan you built looks like.

8
EXECUTE THE PLAN

To build and launch a product with a company of ten is far less complicated than launching a product in a company of 110,000. From supply chain logistics, to product development, to marketing and selling the product internationally, much can go into simply getting a product designed and into the customer's hands. It's no wonder that at a certain point a company shifts the bulk of its efforts away from inventing new products into optimizing the production of its existing products. With everything that goes into execution, efficiencies can be a big boost on anyone's bottom line, driving away the need to take on the risk of focusing on entirely new ways of doing business and instead optimize proven revenue streams. However, remaining in that space means you're left unprepared on how to execute something entirely new in an environment focused on optimizing what's already there. This leaves you in a difficult space when it comes to getting your innovative concept into primetime.

It is inevitable that if you are working on a project requiring more than two layers of management, that it will most likely run over budget and over schedule. A common issue with most enterprises is that when a project has visibility, it gets more attention. Imagine how much attention the Plymouth exhibit would have received from Chrysler at the 1939 World's Fair in order for a car to be assembled as part of the display. The thing with absolute deadlines however, is that things cannot be put on hold in order to tweak or change elements. When an event like the World's Fair occurs, you are building to a deadline. When you look at examples such as the Boeing company, a product can be several years late and be swept under the carpet after all the late fines are written off. An innovative product, something completely new, however, has a great necessity to hit deadlines on time because people will look for any reason to kill a new project. With a new executive in office for example, the quickest way they can make a positive reputation is to cut wasteful spending. Even if this new concept isn't behind schedule, it does not sustain the current business and contribute to streamlining the existing product lines so it is ripe to be cut if things take even a slight downturn. If the executive has their name associated with the project however, and there are ramifications or bragging rights to consider, then micro-management may occur where critical elements are scaled back or eliminated altogether in order to achieve a guaranteed success.

Regardless of what hurdles you are facing in getting this concept built and off the ground, execution will be the greatest challenge you will most likely face because you are doing something that has not been done before. Sure, Chrysler had built Plymouths before and the concept of building a car at an exhibit had even been done by Ford a couple of years earlier, but it took some real brain power to do it in a way that was presentation worthy and ensure a successful product in front of millions of potential customers over the span of the exhibit. This was not disruptive in the sense it was a brand new type of car, or a brand new type of manufacturing. The concept was to display the magic of auto manufacturing so Chrysler incorporated elements like air conditioning for the first time to add to the innovative look and feel of the exhibit. If your concept is to build a new type of car, then build it in a new way that has never been tried, you are most likely not going to show case it on a world's stage.

Getting to the minimal viable product means getting crystal clear on the scope early on, and also knowing during the course of the execution phase what is necessary to keep the soul of the concept intact. If it takes on a life of its own, there is often little that can be done depending on who is calling the shots at that point, but building quick wins in smaller numbers before getting into larger spheres of influence can help you control your ability to execute more effectively.

As we talked about in earlier chapters, building a reputation over time means you will have more control over larger parts of the project as the scope increases on future revisions. This may mean not telling too many people until it is further along, or maybe passing on a project manager that was offered to you so you can keep a closer eye on how the project is moving along. You may need to push back the date to present what you have to your manager because it is not quite where it needs to be to show it to the world.

Start-ups go stealth for the very same reasons, and have invite-only betas to make sure they control the flow of information regarding their product until it is ready for mainstream distribution. In enterprises, this is particularly difficult because there is not a wall of secrecy protecting what it is you are working on, especially if it is a sanctioned project for a world's fair that has a great deal of attention right out of the gate. Whether or not you are a VP with a million dollar budget, or a low level grunt paying your dues in an unrelated job code apart from R&D, there are rules of thumb to consider on how to execute more effectively and avoid the common tangle-ups that projects encounter when being engineered and executed within a company.

Employees Are Consumers First

People fall in and out of love with concepts pretty quickly, and very few have the gumption to go multiple rounds with a concept if it does not directly impact them in some way. Even if an employee is required as part of his or her job to support an initiative, keeping someone motivated is a hard task. Getting buy in and support when it is not a part of their job is even harder, especially when it means the employee has to give up to help support what it is you are trying to pull off. What is even worse is that people have smaller and smaller attention spans, so keeping them motivated and driven can be an uphill battle. Projects don't fall behind or get canceled because the people aren't capable enough, or the executives are not gutsy enough, or there is not enough definition and direction coming out of the process of refining the outcome. Projects fail most often because people lose interest in supporting it or helping to execute on it, which in turn causes the quantitative justifications to arise that justify killing it. When you are doing something edgy and new, people will fall in love with the idea right up until they have to give up something for it, then comes the real test of how your concept stands on its own. Sometimes, motivated teammates can get into a squabble and a few valuable members could end up quitting the project or the company. Perhaps a natural disaster hits, causing a slide in the schedule that sends enthusiasm down and causes a self-perpetuating spiral of missed deadlines to occur, which sparks the ire of upper level management. Though acts of God are certainly out of your control, how you react can adjust as the concept is being executed will be the real measure of how successful the end result will be. Revision triggers happen, and things can occur which you have no control over.

There is something over which you do have control, and that is the staff's interest in the project and how motivated they are to see this concept come to life. If it is just a job for someone, chances are they are comfortable and are willing to allow the project as a whole to go south if it does not have any perceived impact on them. If you think of employees as consumers, then there is no blaming what an employee chooses or does not choose to do, just like you cannot blame a customer for which product they choose to buy or not. Being flexible means you expect things will come up, but you are able to think on your feet and react appropriately as well as anticipate what may come up down the road.

Keeping teammates, volunteers, or direct reports motivated and engaged means leveraging marketing best practices and trying out everything from incentive programs to recognition events along the way so that people feel connected to what it is you are building toward. It would be great to have the flexibility to hand pick the best of the best, as well as be able to let people go for a lack of performance, but you will not always have the ability to pick and choose who ends up driving the most important parts of your concept into fruition.

Spending some time getting to know how a product goes to market, and how companies deal with fickle consumers is going to serve you well when it comes to keeping your own internal teams motivated and driving toward success. Pay and benefits only go so far in keeping someone focused rather than just showing up and doing what they have to do to avoid being fired. Someone might do something out of fear, but people's best work is when they are motivated and not afraid, so focusing on positive results and getting as much effort focused around employees both supporting and helping to create something means they will have a sense of pride and renewed effort when it comes to late nights and working on weekends to hit critical deadlines.

Generalists Versus Specialists

It is often the case that when something exciting comes along, many people want to be involved. It may catch you off guard how people you enjoy working with or respect take an interest in what it is you are doing, and offer to help out in some way, but it is important to recognize which people will actually contribute something meaningful over someone who just wants to be a part of something. Although, having one or two generalists on your project that will span the whole concept beginning to end is important. Mack turned to Duncan, his brother, as he was an accountant that knew finance. If Mack had needed help on graphic design, Duncan may have had an interest in helping put something together, but he would not have been the best go to guy for that role.

When it came to the graphic design, Mack didn't go to a hobbyist because he recognized that having a specialist help on a part time basis was more important than someone playing the role of a generalist trying to figure it out.

Mobile technology was exciting for many people in the companies I worked with, when it came time to develop and move projects forward, there needed to be as few people in the room as possible to get stakeholders on board. Having representatives rather than everyone on the team was often the method I used, even though it would have been fun for everyone to be in on the meeting. Fifteen minute meetings were preferred over sixty minute meetings because the focus was not on hanging out, but on getting an application out the door ahead of schedule and under budget. Those representatives had the most to contribute due to their specialty having the most to do with the mobile project. Although it may hurt some people's feelings to be excluded, it is vital to pick people that have put in the time and effort to be successful before you put them in a role that is undefined, as this concept will cover some uncharted ground. There is no quicker way to un-motivate someone that is great at their job than by putting people on the team that are not able to keep up. There certainly is a time and place for people to learn new skills and be retrained, and to some extent you cannot control who you are paired with, but knowing who the specialists are and making sure the team is set up to succeed is pivotal for the concept to see the light of day.

Iteration

For anyone familiar with Agile development, this is a no-brainer, but in any project, whether focused around software delivery or not, having something viable to show as quickly as possible is critical to continued buy-off for the concept's execution. At my current company, we talk about the 'rule of 90' in that no mobile software project should take longer than 90 days. If the project does take longer then something is at least developed and presentable within that timeframe. Even if it is not the final, having a draft means there is something to look at and evaluate. More often than not, if you can present a clickable prototype of the software application you are looking to build before going to ask for funding, people will react more positively because they have a clear sense of what it is you are building and what they are putting their money toward.

Kickstarter works in a very similar model to this in that the more detail and interaction people have of a project the more likely they are to fund whatever it is you are looking to do. This means that having an early release that is frequently updated along the execution path, will definitely build toward the final release. By this point, you have already presented a prototype and received the backing and funding to begin, so iteration here is more about milestones to demonstrate something useful, to keep both team mates and stakeholders motivated that the project is making progress. If your concept is not a product, or something physical such as a process or a best practice, then get creative and use metaphor and become a bit of a showman. Enthusiasm wanes the longer people go without seeing anything; regardless of what it is your concept is driving toward.

Ongoing Motivation

People are typically motivated by three things and it is important to focus on the things that will keep them engaged beyond simply trying to remain employed.

The first thing is the experience someone could have being tied to a goal. Including people in milestone reviews, as well as making sure members are invited to the launch party, means that each person feels included as a contributing member regardless of their role.

The second thing would be a sense of contributing to something that is bigger than themselves. The Seattle Seahawks are great at this, by playing up the "The 12th Man" concept of each fan being a member of the team and giving the fans themselves their own jersey number – the number 12. Each person on a team can often feel marginalized in light of a larger project, so finding ways to make each person feel included is critical at each step of the project.

The third and final thing would be an incentive in the form of something physical that has symbolic or actual value. This could be anything from corporate swag with the product branding, to an early prototype of the product itself.

Focusing on any one of those three aspects will help you keep people engaged throughout the project, and help the motivation stay at the same level throughout the execution.

Experience

Using the experience as a motivation means drawing the team members into what it is they are contributing to and how they have a unique role to play on the team they are on. If you were building a concept for something as monumental as the World's Fair, this is already baked into the project, but having something brought up about the work they are doing and what kind of positive experience it is or will be someday when employees look back means that showing up and working on this project each day has an experiential benefit beyond the project itself and carries some unique value. If it's not glamorous work, then discussing the experience they will have once it is over can help. There will be an experiential element to what the team is working on, and talking about the current or future experience will go a long way to helping draw more motivation during the execution phases. For stakeholders, it is likely that the experience will not be the prime motivator for backing the project. By describing to them the experience of being the brave and the few, stakeholders who back such a grand endeavor will most likely turn the others around to support you when you start saying things like "grand endeavor" in milestone reviews.

Cause

This does not apply to backing corporate concepts the majority of the time, but is at least worth noting in the event your concept does have altruistic purposes attached to it.

Many people are motivated by something that has purpose beyond just having a financial or survival goal around it. Perhaps the project isn't particularly humanitarian, but being cause motivated could mean that the concept has a larger purpose beyond the goals established in sponsorship. Most often, the cause is going to be qualitative and add to whatever quantitative benefits the concept has on its own.

Incentive

The most obvious motivation is going to be incentive based, where stakeholders and team members have a tangible incentive to see this project completed. It could be a quarterly bonus tied to the successful completion of the concept, or perhaps a promotion tied to launching the concept into the company's product group. Chances are the potential disruption this concept will have, that makes it so innovative to begin with, will not produce immediate benefits to the group. Even when people are supporting what they are creating, there will be times that challenge them to continue supporting the initiative. Having something tangible is far more powerful than something that is conceptual and theoretical.

Almost as important, are the talking points during stakeholder conversations. Your stakeholders are going to be motivated by one or more of these three things, so understanding what drives each of the stakeholders will help in addressing the project during milestone reviews. Keep in mind, the more the stakeholders are tied in the more likely they are to continue supporting the project when it hits a bump or two along the way.

9
MEDIATE THE DIALOGUE

At this point in the process, the hard work of getting the project is done and it is time to do the final read out for buy-off on all the stakeholders and influencers that will take what you have done and make decisions on what to do with it. Whether it is the board you are presenting to as the CEO, or your direct leadership finding the output of the project you have put time into, it's the roadshow that will quickly turn into a crossroad.

After the execution is done and the various versions are being presented, how do you handle the input? How do you stage the meetings? When discussing the concept in milestone meetings, regardless of how far along the concept is, it is still considered by most to be in draft mode. Once you are completed and are presenting it to the larger audience for the final product demonstration, then you should expect a whole new type of feedback. When people have the sense that something is in process, they will react differently and most will not give honest feedback because people do not like being critical face to face. However, that much needed critical feedback may come out when the concept is released into the wild, which is why there are multiple versions often released past the beta phase of a software release. You will never get everything right out of the gate, even with focus groups and stakeholder reviews, and that is okay. The nice thing about launching a concept into an enterprise is that you aren't judged on sales numbers; however, you also do not have the same type of feedback you would were you measuring how fast it flew off the shelves. If this is the kind of concept you are looking to launch into the product space, as something sold to consumers, then you probably already have a great deal of processes in place on how this will work. If this is the case, there may be a soft launch internally as well as a pilot phase you will want to take advantage of before any major roll out. I will not go into how to launch a product (that's a book in and of itself), but will include helpful top of mind things to consider once the concept is built and it is ready to be launched.

Apps + Innovations & Angry Birds

If you played video games in the early 90's, you may recall the game Scorched Earth written by Wendell Hicken back in the DOS era. The purpose of the game was to take turns between two tanks using different types of munitions to blow up the other tank. The control you had was essentially the height of the cannon barrel to get just the right trajectory for the ammo. There were options for different types of weapons and shells in later editions, and the game went through a number of revisions. No one would have thought the concept might be used to launch a bird out of a catapult to attack a bunch of pigs and become the Mario Brothers of mobile gaming. Yet, Angry Birds has spawned everything from gummy candies to stuffed toys and a number of sequels focused around launching those birds out of a catapult with much less sophistication than Scorched Earth had later in its life. Even if Scorched Earth were not shareware it did not create such a movement. Remember, being innovative and disruptive does not mean creating something completely new. A great quote from "*Innovator's DNA*" says, "Questioning. Innovators are consummate questioners who show a passion for inquiry. Their queries frequently challenge the status quo, just as Jobs did when he asked, 'Why does a computer need a fan?' They love to ask, 'If we tried this, what would happen?₄" Innovators, like Jobs, ask questions to understand how things really are today, why they are that way, and how they might be changed or disrupted."

When you are discussing the concept with individuals, and demonstrating the finished project, keep in mind that not everyone in the room is going to have the right mindset when it comes to appreciating or even conceiving what it is you are going for. It doesn't mean it is wrong, but being a good salesperson means relating the concept to the right context and helping each individual grasp onto what it is you are sharing. Sometimes the best medicine needs a peanut butter and jelly sandwich, to get people to swallow it. In the Book "*Innovator's Way*", author Peter J. Denning describes the different traits that make up an innovator based on the research his team conducted. "We found that the innovators' practices fall into eight categories:

1. Sensing
2. Envisioning
3. Offering
4. Adopting (first time)
5. Sustaining
6. Executing
7. Leading
8. Embodying₅"

Notice that sales person is not anywhere in the list, but leading is. To lead is to be out in front, and sometimes it means trusting the direction you are heading in long enough for others to follow. However, when you are mediating dialog on the concept and stakeholders' buy-off is essential for moving the initiative forward, consider how relating what it is stakeholders care about in a way that acts as a bridge will help. Sometimes getting people to buy-off on a concept, for instance pigs and birds, means finding previous examples that had similar components focused around tanks and shells. To gain enough buy-off to move it forward, make sure you always undersell on what the upside is because you cannot truly predict when you have a great game versus a mobile revolution in gaming on your hands.

Leverage Your Protagonist

In every meeting people assume a role in the context of the presentation. You have the audience and the presenter, and the presenter has the role of portraying a certain amount of knowledge to gain buy-off on what is being said. Imagine that you are in a play and you are trying to stir the emotions of the audience in such a way as to sway them all in the same direction. What theatrics could you deploy to paint a clear picture without drawing out a large fictional narrative? Being the protagonist sometimes simply means describing an antagonist that everyone can understand and collectively despise. Perhaps your concept is a car window that de-ices itself. If you live in Wisconsin, you just have to share stories of when you had to pull over to chip the ice off your windshield wipers because it was so cold driving that the wipers themselves would collect ice. Everyone that has driven in freezing temperatures has experienced that at least once, and has a collective agreement that it is a hassle. Assuming you have buy-off and you are the hapless victim to the mean and vicious ice, then people in the audience are more likely to follow the dialog through the concept's introduction and request for moving the concept forward.

Build the Curve

Sometimes building a new concept in a company is ahead of its time, and does not have a reference model or something to relate to what it is you are presenting. This usually doesn't make it past the concept stage, but assuming you have made it this far it is now up to you to convince the prospective stakeholders or clients that are hearing about the concept for the first time to buy off on the finished product. If this is the case, you need to build your own curve and create an adoption curve of whatever it is you are showing off. For example, a roll of toilet paper that never runs out because it is made of nano-robotic synthetic generators is not something people will have a strong context and understanding around, but the concept in theory sounds interesting so maybe you will gain buy-off on it. Obviously, that example has easy empathy for people to get behind, but there is so much that is unproven with nano-bots that people might feel uncomfortable being the one to try it for the first time. Demonstrating how the early adopters of nano-bots have them inserted into various parts of their body to help with blood clotting easily demonstrates the safety of nano-technology and that this is a proven technology that has found a more practical every day application. Make sure you aren't fabricating your own facts when you do this. Relating something new to something that is already in place can help build a curve and create a sense of confidence that you are not completely out of your mind, just someone who thinks outside the box within range of the box itself.

You +/- Your Audience

The thing you have in common with your audience is that you both care enough about the concept to show up to the presentation. For you, hopefully your excitement is a no-brainer, but the audience is going to be at different levels of enthusiasm. Getting everyone on board from the get-go was easier, because you have little to lose and everything to gain from getting buy-off and support for going out and developing the concept to begin with. However, once the concept is complete then there is much more to lose if the output turns the hearts and minds of those same sponsors away, or creates a disconnect around those that just heard of the concept for the first time. Keep in mind that you will always be the most convinced that this is a good idea, and it always helps to have confidence, but you must also not become too confident in the innovative idea you are putting forward that you disenfranchise those in your audience.

Encouraging questions that may or may not make sense is a good idea, but scoffing at a question that indicates someone in the audience doesn't get it means you better have an alternate option for moving forward. Having user empathy and working to bridge your concept and their understanding in a way that is not condescending is critical to gaining support, regardless of how good your idea is. Oftentimes when a corporation buys a company, they are as interested if not more so in the people than the product itself. Regardless of what it is you are promoting, if you are a jerk then people will be less inclined to support whatever it is, and if they have the strings to pull to make this concept go from project complete to revolutionary game changer, then doing whatever you have to stay on good terms is critical.

The Good, the Bad, and the Ugly

Even you will be asked to look back on the process it took you to get to this point, and will no doubt have a multitude of regrets and things you could have done differently, it is important to emphasize the fact that the concept has been completed and that you have learned much in the process of engineering the idea into its final state. Reflecting too much on the negative will erode confidence, and there is certainly a time and place to fess up and share the post-mortem.

However, when presenting the output of the concept, you want to not downplay, but simply avoid talking about the negatives of the project. If asked, don't shrug off the question; remember that there is an optimistic and positive way to answer any question. You may mess up one or two meetings during the roadshow, and it most likely won't be enough to sink you, but make sure to take notes and understand the feedback you are getting from everyone to change how you present the concept and what you will do differently the next time. Take notes, making sure people have a sense you are doing just that, because the concept is never really done, even if what you are presenting is a final product. People will become more engaged with what it is you are showing them if you make it a conversation less about the concept itself, but how each individual in the room has a valid opinion and their input is important. Not talking down to your audience may be common sense, but even having an aura around you that says you are the innovator, and they are a necessary evil can have a big impact on how you are appearing to come off. Too often, people will get to 99 yards and sabotage themselves during the last yard because they have a preconceived notion that things will go in a certain direction. If you are nervous about the meeting, practice enough to get rid of the nervousness and walk in knowing the material, and knowing it in such a way that you can focus on the audience and making the monologue more of a dialog. Knowing the names of the people in the room and stopping the presentation to make sure everyone is tracking what you are saying, are all critical for having a clear sense of the pulse and how it will impact the next steps for the concept.

Even though this is the end of the battle, the war will still have to be fought. You have played this part of the project to its end, but the concept has a long way to go before being disruptive and really changing the course of the river. In the book, "*The Myths of Innovation*", Scott Berkun outlines what it takes to give an effective idea,

Step 1: Refine your idea
Step 2: Shape your pitch
Step 3: Follow the power
Step 4: Start with their perspective
Step 5: Make three pitches
Step 6: Test the pitch
Step 7: Deliver (a pitch is a performance)
Step 8: Learn from failure
Step 9: Go your own way.

At some point, you have to recognize that even with all the great feedback in the world, you come to a crossroad where you will have to deviate from the pack and continue doing things a little bit differently. After all, if anyone in the audience had it nailed then they would be presenting their ideas instead of listening to your presentation, and no one will understand the concept to the level that you will grasp it.

Expecting everyone to jump on board right away of course is not realistic either, and the same is true for the process to follow. You are going to have to figure out what comes next on your own to some degree. Do you go back to the drawing board? Do you scrap the idea? Even if funding is killed and the project is handed off to another divisional chair, you will still have something in the concept you brought to life and it is your responsibility to adapt and continue to grow it. It could be time for another bootstrapped initiative done off hours and may never see another conference room until it is further along, or perhaps it's a lesson to improve on how you sell and not simply improving what you sell.

At this phase, it is important to recognize that too often people will leave companies and go out on their own because it's easier to innovate with a team of five people you helped put together that are already driven, focused, and funded to get something new off the ground. If those stars line up for you, being an entrepreneur is a great way to go and a worthy pursuit for anyone that can pull it off. However, there will be a whole new set of problems to face and challenges to conquer, and not every start-up turns into a disruptive powerhouse. If you are not in a place you can cut down drastically on how much you spend, do not want to take on the risk, or simply do not have the connections to make it happen then it is something you can work toward over time. At this point, you are in a position on your journey where you have gotten an 'atta boy', handed off the work and, are perhaps, starting on a new task. Maybe it is something you can continue with, but with restrictions and greater oversight. Every once in a while it turns into the opportunity of a lifetime, and the promotion you have dreamed of. However, corporations largely work in patterns and rhythms and disruption is often considered a young man's game.

Too often the greatest ideas are left up to those with the least amount of vision to command, and it is reducing the risk and creating a clear path towards profitability that leaves companies in the state they are in. Innovations will continue as pet projects, and R&D has a high rate of vaporware along with millions spent on patent counter-measures and legal protections. I emphasize this here in the book because it is the most likely place you will settle and slink back into the corporate ether you rose from to get to where you are. It will be very hard to push the disruption past the point where people's toes are getting stepped on; because the more people that get involved the harder it will be to keep pushing up hill. However, this is where an innovator's grit is proven and legends are made. CEOs that can throw out the status quo and really shake things up don't follow a playbook in order to determine how to succeed, but they put the right things in place to make sure they have done everything they can to avoid failing.

As with anything great, it will be difficult to pull off. Your company doesn't see the value in mobile devices, even after you have given the final read-out on your time-motion study showing direct Return On Investment (ROI)? It isn't that mobile devices are not useful, but there was something more important than ROI keeping those folks in the room pulling the trigger. Your presentation was a hit, but now there's a committee set up to assess and standardize mobile for corporate use? Avoid getting tied down in committee meetings. Instead push to find quick-to-launch use cases that generate buzz for the types of quick wins you will need to get enough user adoption in place for mobile to really take off. This will create a greater sense of urgency for the committee to pull a plan together quickly and get solutions out the door. Governance of course has a place, but learn to recognize when it can turn into unnecessary process and procedure, and avoid getting sucked into meetings that produce results at a glacial rate.

Finally, make sure you are taking everything you learn in the read-outs for this and organize it in a way that is going to provide the most reuse down the road. The next chapter will talk about deconstructing the output, and how to gain the most re-use from what it is you have just gone through. This will help you to repeat the process and make sure you are in a constant state of evolution as it could take several concepts to really hone your skill and get through the kinds of barriers all too common in a corporate setting.

10
DECONSTRUCT THE OUTPUT

When breaking down the outcome of your concept's execution, were you on the offensive, preempting what you anticipated the enterprise reaction to your concept would be? Revision triggers will come from many different directions, and if you are working in an offensive capacity preparing yourself for what's to come around the corner then you will be in a better position to handle whatever comes your way. Being corrective, which is acting defensively based on what is happening in the present, will cost time and effort that you may not have to spare. Think of the cost of fire prevention versus firefighting. Here you have the opportunity to not only consider where your project may trip up, where you can begin to engineer the right steps to put in place and make sure along the way that you are setting yourself up to anticipate and stay one step ahead of potential issues. Does your projector often fail? Consider printouts prior to the big board meeting. Does your sponsor only like ideas they come up with? Think of an indifferent approach for presenting your concept proposal. If this were a start-up, you would have no illusions that those inside your company and outside your company have two very difference perceptions of the value of your concept. Consider how working on a team within an enterprise has that same truth behind those supporting you and those whose support you are looking to gain. If we build on concepts taken from the book "*Super-flexibility for Knowledge Enterprises*", we can begin to see how this can take place.

Principle #1: Strategizing for Maneuvering

The first principle focuses on how you react to revision triggers, and helps you identify whether you're thinking and reacting defensively when revision triggers occur today or whether you're on the offensive preparing for what's to come. When you're going through the process of executing the concept, at which points did you run into resistance from people acting defensively? Has this caused a corrective, or "firefighting" mentality in the past versus being pre-emptive in a state of fire prevention? Though it's easier to prevent fires than put them out, many companies run into the trap of only responding and correcting problems when they occur versus working to prevent them. Oftentimes, you'll see resistance coming from persons based on a desire to minimize risks on unknown variables or they may see something new introduced as unnecessary or secondary to the goals or targets at hand. It's often the case that a company focused too much on firefighting won't take the time to prevent future fires and will therefore be in a constant state of survival. A human body can reject a transplanted heart, because it's identified as foreign even though it's necessary to sustain that body. Just the same, a company needs new and sometimes risky ideas to maneuver around obstacles and respond appropriately to things that affect the company. As you deconstruct the outcome, pay close attention to where you see these types of defensive barriers raise themselves, whether it's overly cumbersome paperwork or difficulty getting executive buy-off, and consider how you can better prepare to take these challenges head on for the next go-round.

Principle #2: Executing by Recalibrating

In the course of executing the concept, were there bad

ideas that were kept for too long? Were there adaptations or modifications that slowed down the project, and kept progress from occurring sooner? In thinking about the steps to getting something new going inside your company, it is hard enough to get a minimal viable product out the door without excess functions, features, or modifications. Vetting ideas often, and disposing of the lion's share is a much more effective approach than keeping every idea in the work stream and waiting to see what comes out in the wash. If an idea passes muster through the first round of review, sit on it for a day and see if it's still a good one the next. Most stand-up comedians come up with hundreds of jokes, but famous television comedians such as Stephen Colbert or Jay Leno will have writers write up hundreds of jokes, then see if they are still funny days later, after the initial punch line is told.

If your idea still holds water, elevate it and get people involved outside of the initial conversation to take a look and vet it again. If it is still looking solid, add it to the project as a recalibration of the initial concept rather than as something entirely new. If it doesn't fit with the current project, or threatens to delay progress, then consider it a revision for a later date. It is critical to be aware of what a recalibration looks like over a spin-off into another project. Consider how this change will impact the overall progress of the project under way, how the outcome will be improved or diminished because of these changes, and if this is something that may enhance but also delay the milestone, thereby negating any positive outcome the addition may have had. Keep in mind that one missed deadline is a much bigger deal than a typical 'nice-to-have' feature. Thinking back on the project, were there changes made that could have waited? Was there anything introduced as a change request or suggestion that jeopardized the deadline? How many ideas were considered new projects and spun off as such rather than incorporating them into the existing concept? It is important to have a clear sense of how many all-nighters were required as a result of this, and if it will impact sponsorship or participation from willing employees in future initiatives. Finishing something by the skin of your teeth may give you an adrenaline rush, but it's a sure fire way to appear reckless or mismanaged for future concepts.

Principle #3: Organizing by Federating

Most employees consider the impact the organizational structure of their company makes on things like sponsorship, or the "way decisions are made around here," when it comes to things like tribal leaders, the power of shoulder tapping, and which senior leader is on the outs with executive management or not. However, when you consider the cohesive aspect (personality), clustering aspect (anatomy), and connective aspect (circulation) of a company as a single federated group of traits, then the understanding you have of the company can take on a new direction. For example, only considering the anatomy of a company as having a flat management structure may cause you to think that senior leaders are fairly approachable for new ideas. But, the personality of the company could be very conservative and the circulation will cause the first hint of an innovative and disruptive concept to cycle through the organization with a strong disapproval for any executive that considers funding it.

Having a clear sense of how these aspects are federated together will give you a much more comprehensive view of the organization you are working within to see this concept come to light. Thinking back on the project, where did some aspect of the organization trip you up? Did some aspect of the conversations you were having about sponsorship, or the status of the meeting catch you off guard? Did requirements for staffing the team strike you as nonsensical, and did you run into any significant roadblocks because of cultural aspects that had nothing to do with the anatomy or circulation of the organization? When you have all three of these aspects in mind, understanding the complexity of the organization you are looking to maneuver through can greatly help your chances of being successful.

Principle #4: Leading by Aligning

In most situations when it comes to aligning a team, and building your stakeholder group, you are going to hone in on the anatomy of an organization to help you make decisions around who can sign off on what amount, which individuals have the most power over certain decisions, and what alignment of positions makes the most sense to staff and execute on your initiative. If you consider a parent/child relationship in your organization, you will often run into procedures, binary thinking, monologue oriented meetings, and people focused on compliance and checking off the boxes. However, treating everyone involved in the project as a peer and facilitating peer to peer interactions regardless of the level of the individual, will not only facilitate a customized approach focused on outcome, but also create a team that generates commitment, is dialog oriented, and takes on a multi-faceted approach because this is a structure people are not programmed to react to. Making a rule that all team meetings strip people of their rank and role when they walk in, and that they are there because they have something valuable to contribute as well as obtaining the buy-in required to move the project forward, means you are creating the kind of conversations where everyone will contribute. Thinking back on the project, were there times when different groups disconnected? Was there a breakdown in meetings that caused emotional responses to otherwise uncomplicated issues? Did you have to halt the project at some point because you had a team member who was asked to leave, or one who resigned? Did stakeholders at any point withdraw their support due to a miscommunication? Gaining this kind of group dynamic will not only solve common teaming issues, but will also ensure individuals involved in the project will spend energy working to resolve their issues because they feel as though they will miss something important to them if they withdraw and walk away. The more of an attachment someone has to something, the stronger the bond and buy-in to create the type of environment where even the nastiest conflicts can be worked through.

Principle #5: Organizing by Recycling

Even you may be looking to incorporate a disruptive concept, using techniques that have not been tried in the company before, or teams that are marching somewhat to the beat of their own drum, there will still be certain techniques that have worked in prior initiatives with proven results. After all, the company is still cranking out existing products and making revenue, so something is most likely going right. If things are going right to some extent, the people on your team, as well as the stakeholders supporting you, will most likely already have an understanding of how things go, except for the occasional new employee or outsourced resource. If the process in place works, then consider how it can be folded into what you are proposing to do.

During the project, did you leverage best practices from around the company to complete your concept? Did you build a lot of new resources from scratch, or did you re-engineer existing tools used in projects you have worked on in the past? Did roles and responsibilities start with a template from elsewhere in the company? Or did you delay the project, spending time trying to get everyone aligned on a new system and structure? Sometimes being disruptive means doing things differently, especially inside corporations, but not everything has to be redone and sometimes it is important to take a hard look at how much has to be done from scratch before you put down the wish list for sponsorship. Not only will it save money to reuse what is already out there, it will also save precious time before a minimal viable product is out the door and ready to demonstrate. On your first project, consider yourself cash poor regardless of the budget, and be scrappy without risking deadlines. The rewards will come when you have launched something completely new in the enterprise under budget and on time.

These principles are far from comprehensively

addressing each and every issue you will run into, but putting them all together as a postmortem for your project can help you identity some of the root issues that tend to affect organizations working on being flexible and rapidly adopting to change. Whether it is considering how maneuverability could have helped you reduce supply chain issues and logistical challenges, or better understanding the stakeholder feedback by looking at the team through the federating lens, having a sense for how these principles can apply to your concept ahead of time means you are more likely to anticipate revision triggers and be preemptive from the get-go.

Because you are reading this, I will venture to say, that you have probably completed at least one project in your life before now. Start by taking these principles and put your previous experiences through these filters. What things are you seeing for the first time? What aspects do you feel these principles miss? If there is a big blind spot in your analysis, consider what principle you might add to this list to help you in future projects. The goal is not to give you a 10-step formula, and shove every enterprise example into it, but rather to set you up with a framework that has worked many times over for companies. I will leave it up to you, the reader, to evolve this to suit your needs. The moment something is written down, it becomes dated, and it's from that point forward that it will continue to become out of date in some fashion or another. However, the truth that formed a piece of writing can last well beyond the relevance of the work itself, so consider taking these principles outside of this context into other areas of your professional life and see what you come up with.

Deconstructing the output implies a necessity for taking good notes from the get-go; so don't wait until the very end of a project to start to look back on each aspect of it. Meeting minutes may seem excessive, but capturing key moments in the project or key quotes spoken by a stakeholder can offer up context into the direction the project ended up taking. Leveraging a note taking tool such as OneNote or Evernote, or perhaps using Microsoft Project to keep track of the project itself, can all aid in helping you improve on what you have done. Whether it's Version 2 you are ramping up for, or a whole new concept than the one you just finished, having a mentality of constant improvement means you are paying attention to more than deadlines and signatures, but have a holistic sense of the process itself. Yes, the stakeholder did agree over a beer to support your project, but what was it that you said that worked? Was it nuance, or something a little more methodological behind how you approached it? If it worked, did it work elsewhere? What made you feel this was the concept to pursue? How did that process and approach work out? Could any snags along the way to sponsorship, have been avoided? Being disruptive can take time and energy, and may take several revisions to get something out the door, but being effective is something everyone is capable of and will take multiple tries to get right. No one has something as complex as an enterprise down pat the moment they walk in the door because it is full of people who are loosely coupled with rules, responsibilities and desires. Regardless of the vertical, it will take time to make an impact, especially if it is disruptive.

Once you have had success in understanding how your project operated, and have take-aways on moving onto the next project, then you are ready to re-construct the process for a second go.

11
REPEAT THE PROCESS

In the book "*Mastery*", George Leonard discussed the principle that mastery was only possible once you have achieved some level of success doing something, then continue to do it thousands of times until you get better in that one area and plateau. The process will continue on several more times, because absolute mastery is never possible, you will always be improving in new ways. Mr. Leonard uses the example of learning tennis swings, and discusses how a tennis player will practice different parts of their swing, mastering each aspect, the back hand for example, only after they have done it several thousand times, before moving on to the next part of the swing. This is a particularly important factor to consider because it makes the case that getting good at something takes time, but becoming a master of something is a lifelong pursuit.

To effectively change an enterprise can take several years, and making a career out of it may take a lifetime. The enterprise arena is changing drastically, from technology change to the people that show up to work every day, and the pace of change is not likely to slow down. Every so many thousand years, civilization makes a shift in cultural attributes. Every so many hundred years, technology will evolve into different ages. Every ten years, society will change demographically. Every five to seven years, technology will cause corporations to become disrupted in some way. I do not think it is a stretch to say that each of those changes are lining up more rapidly now than usual, and this affects every aspect of the human experience. You cannot definitively say things are shifting that drastically until we look back once it is over. When you consider how the generational shift is influencing the work place with people that have never known a world without the internet, airplanes, or the ability to contact anyone in the world at any point, you can see that inevitably there will be new innovations in a world built on that kind of foundation. These things have never before happened in human civilization, and it is creating a platform to build entirely new things from.

Yet, in some ways, enterprises are at a disadvantage because to really take advantage of these changes requires the ability to shift quickly and drastically, which leads to the ideal state for being able to handle these changes. If you have worked for a single enterprise your whole life, you will no doubt have a very clear understanding of all the levers and mechanisms making up the company you work for and be able to recount stories of "how things used to go." You know how different things are from ten years ago, and yet also recognize how similar things may be at the same time. "The way we do things" is a powerful force inside any enterprise, and forms the cultural fabric that keeps any executive from coming in and shaking things up too drastically. The immune system of a company is to protect it from drastic shifts in direction, and ensure that the lights still turn on every morning. This is especially true in a public company where drastic corporate shifts will affect volatility and create unease with the board if anything too drastic takes place. As the age -old adage goes, when you put a frog in a pot of water and turn up the heat quickly, the frog will jump out of the pot. However, if you slowly turn up the heat, the frog will stay there and cook.

Companies that used to be on the forefront of technology innovation, such as Kodak, are going bankrupt, because they fail to grasp the disruptive force and evolve accordingly. They stayed in the pot, so to speak, rather than jumping out into a new business strategy. Even though Kodak is now emerging from bankruptcy, no one would have thought bankruptcy was even possible for Kodak 20 years ago. How does a company that creates an entire industry collapse under the weight of change without being able to change itself? Can any company consider itself safe once it owns the marketplace for a particular product, and if so for how long is it safe? Much like a forest, some trees die so that others can leech off the nutrients and grow in its place.

Steve Jobs worked at Hewlett-Packard as an intern prior to starting Apple, and in 2012, Apple was in a decidedly different economic position than Hewlett-Packard. It wasn't because Hewlett-Packard was unaware of what Apple had been up to, or that they had fallen asleep at the wheel. Apple had been in a poor state itself back in 1997 when Microsoft bailed the competitor out. Since then, Apple has gone on to become one of the most valuable companies in the world and a market leader in mobile, with Microsoft working to regain its market share in the mobile space. This dance will continue on, with one company replacing the next, companies like Apple leading the market in photography while former market leaders in photography, such as Kodak, enter bankruptcy because the market for casual photography now belongs to mobile device companies. It is a dance that will continue to twist, because change is inevitable, regardless of how executives respond to it.

Becoming a master at disruptive innovation is easier in the enterprise because it is constantly being disrupted whether or not you are at the wheel doing anything. Companies may fight change, but the world will continue to change with or without their permission, leaving them in last place if they do not adapt and stay relevant. If you asked someone at Kodak in the 1940's if they were worried about the company going bankrupt, I imagine they would have given you a puzzled look and pointed out the number of people taking photos as proof of their success both past and present. More people today take pictures than ever before, it is just that they do not use Kodak products to do so. The human experience will always be captured to some extent, people have not stopped writing down their thoughts, but have simply changed from stone to animal skin to pen and paper to keyboards and tablets.

Discovering how your concept fits in is the key to understanding the undercurrent of change occurring within the company you work for, and then working to gain clear knowledge of what your company is doing to adapt to the current times. No corporation goes out of business for a lack of effort or awareness of what's happening. But if a company that specializes in railroad equipment keeps building railroad equipment when everyone else in the transportation industry has moved onto airplanes, then it will have a tough time competing no matter what it does because it's focused too much on the product the company builds (trains) and not the purpose of the company itself (transporting people in the most efficient way possible). If you talk to someone at Toyota, they will tell you that the purpose of the company is not to build cars but build effective methods for personal transportation. Toyota may stop building cars if the most effective method for personal transportation is no longer an automobile, based on the parameters they have determined as to what defines effective methods. Rather than continuing to try to build a better car, Toyota is setting itself to master transportation regardless of the method in which they use to accomplish that goal. If General Electric only stuck to generating electricity or building better light bulbs, they may still be in business, but would look drastically different from where they are today.

To master disruption is like mastering the art of bull riding. You may become good, and even master it, but everyone has the potential to get bucked off if you drop your focus for even a moment because bulls do not cater to any individual and no two bulls are exactly alike. Disruptive forces have no master, and no company is safe because they are a revered brand, or have been in business for hundreds of years. If you are working at an enterprise, you are riding the bull with your career each day you walk into work. You may have more or less control over the bull depending on where you sit in the company, but you will make personal decisions that can affect the company for the better, or worse, depending on how you chose to act. No tennis player begins their career on the world stage, but every tennis player begins with a racket, a ball, and the ability to practice and determine the level of dedication they are willing to contribute to the game. There will be factors outside of each players control as to how competitive they will end up being, and how far they'll go, but even the players with the best potential can end up second rate if they do not fully commit themselves to mastery. Change is inevitable, and someone will crack the nut helping your company keep its leading edge or be the founder of the company that replaces it. You have the opportunity right now to be someone that commits yourself to being a successful innovator, which helps your company adapt to the current climate, and works past the barriers that keep most enterprises from moving forward. You might not be the next Steve Jobs, but you can surpass all the people that check into their jobs every day and resign themselves to letting change happen to them rather than standing in the path of change and helping those around them adapt in turn. There will be great barriers put in place that will prevent you from being successful, and it will feel like riding a bull sometimes, but mastery means you will keep getting back up and doing it a thousand more times until you have mastered just one aspect, so you can then begin on the next aspect and continue on.

As you achieve mastery, you will gain a sense of premonition. You will be able to anticipate where the ball is going to land on your side of the court in the blink of an eye, and be able to react one or two milliseconds faster than your competitor who doesn't have quite the level of mastery that you do. But it is enough to score the point and win the match. If you have your back turned to the court, no matter how good you are, you are going to miss the ball each and every time. It may seem obvious that any tennis player would pay attention to where the ball is headed, and that their opportunity to succeed comes in how they react to what they think it is going to do, but they also have the benefit of knowing the ball has only so many places it can land and the relative direction it will head in based on how it's hit. Most tennis players know when they hit the ball in a certain way they will elicit a predicted response and increase their chances of getting the opponent to mess up. If it were as easy as more practice then there would be little point to the game. In the enterprise arena, you cannot always predict how people will react to a product, or gain a crystal clear idea of how companies can stay competitive regardless of how many books and studies are done on the subject. I am sure Kodak hired some smart people to help the company change direction, and yet they still found themselves in the situation they were in. We cannot know every conversation that was had behind closed doors, but we can study what decisions they made along the way and use it as a lesson to grow from.

Studying the hard drive industry, Clayton Christenson was able to determine that enterprises were better at sustaining innovations than disruptive ones, because the hard drive industry changed so quickly that you could study the entire evolution of a company in considerably less time than a company like Kodak, and there are legitimate reasons why companies continue to do what they do and do not abandon ship to avoid taking on water. Stephen Elop, in 2011, wrote a memo describing Nokia as being on a burning platform and the drastic move to go all in with Windows Phone while discontinuing Symbian was necessary to stay afloat and evolve into a competitive company. As I write this, it is still up in the air on what will happen to Nokia, but it is a great example of a company that recognized it should not focus on sustaining innovations and slight evolutions of the same platform and that a drastic change was necessary to stay afloat. Sometimes it is painful to work in a new direction, and shifting a company's focus is no small feat. However, being pre-emptive means starting the change before it requires a drastic press release or a last minute effort to avoid bankruptcy.

Rules for sports such as baseball and tennis may change over time; often playing for several years will cause minor adjustments at best. With technology, however, the rules of the road change much more often and require a level of agility far above most other professions. Whether it's adopting a new programming language, going from on - premise administration to cloud computing, or phasing out laptops for tablets, the shift in technology can often overtake even the most amply prepared technologist if they are too focused on the technology and tools, and not on the trends and impacts. Much like the example of Toyota adapting the transportation they are providing, if you are focused on providing the best method to access and interact with information and data versus providing the best laptop support, or building the best COBOL applications, then you will be in a much better position to adapt and change with the technology shift. Repeating the process will not look the same each year, and will need to evolve with each project you do, and each concept you push forward, because it is a wave you will constantly have to stay on top of.

The thing that changes much slower than technology is the people who are using the solutions. Regardless of how rapidly technology shifts, people have likes and dislikes that will change at a slower pace and will always be the real indicator of how successful a disruptive concept is inside a corporation. People will want to feel included in communities, will want to be acknowledged for their contribution, and will always push back on something if they feel threatened by it. By understanding people, and the impacts disruption has on them, you will have a better opportunity to be preemptive when it comes to building a strategy on how to approach the stakeholders and team members you will be working with, working for, and gaining buy-off from. You will not need to earn a minor in sociology, but learning to pay attention to the human element of what it is you are doing will matter more than the viability of the concept itself at times. After all, if people don't understand or do not like what it is you are pitching, it will not matter how amazing it is on paper or how much you think it will improve the bottom line. Much like invading a castle, the problem is not scaling the wall or breaking down the gate, but watching out for the arrows being flung at you or the soldiers charging at you that will make the biggest difference. Real strategy only considers the tools to a small extent, but focuses more on the human element. Whether it's reading The Art of War, playing poker, or performing a magic trick, it all comes down to how you understand and interact with the people around you that will make or break you.

As you focus on building a process you can repeat, focus on getting better with the people you are working with. If you notice there are one or two people in the audience that will matter more than the others, make sure they have bought off on the concept prior to the meeting. Social engineering is critical, PowerPoint presentations are optional. It's not manipulation as much as it is taking into account that there are people on the opposite side of the boardroom and they operate with personalities, likes and dislikes, and triggers.

Making a company work better, means the people in the company work better, and having an understanding of how your concept will improve the company means you can make it clear how the employees themselves will improve because of it. When it comes to lobbying in congress, I would bet that lobby organizations know how many votes they do or do not have prior to the vote, and will work with one congressman at a time to get the consensus they need before the vote shows up rather than waiting to make a splash on the day of the vote. There's always a margin of error, because people can change their mind at the last minute, but taking the handful of impactful stakeholders out for coffee one-on-one prior to the big meeting to ask how they feel about the concept, and what they would change, means you have a better opportunity to explain the concept and gain their buy-off and in turn, everyone can teach you something. Tailoring is just one of the many things you will get better at as you continue to launch concepts in an enterprise.

Being open to input and being humble can make a big impact out of the gate as well, and even with ten wins under your belt there should still be a sense that you have not perfected anything yet. There is no tennis player who cannot lose a match regardless of how good they are, so always make sure to check your ego at the door. This may sound like common sense to you, but too often I have seen subject matter experts who are validated by their immediate peers step into another part of the enterprise and be taken down ten or more notches by an executive that has not worked with them before, doesn't understand their brilliance, and really wants nothing to do with whatever it was they just presented. If you feel like you have the ego thing down, then you do not have the ego thing down. Having some small level of fear going into each meeting will keep you honest, and help you to better understand that at any point you could say or do the wrong thing, with even with the best intentions and preparation.

Being honest, treating people with respect and approaching each meeting and one-on-one with the same level of appreciation for the person or people you are speaking with will help them be more receptive to the groundbreaking stuff you are presenting. Furthermore, they will be more honest with you if you are honest with them, so dropping the facade and being real is a great way to pull the bullets out of people's guns, and disarm a potentially hostile situation. Everyone likes something, and no one hates absolutely everything, so sometimes simply asking someone what they want to see and how they want to approach what it is you are developing can be much more effective than trying to manipulate and maneuver. Manipulation is slimy at worst, sneaky at best, and treats everyone like you are selling them when what you are really trying to do is improve the company, improve the environment, and disrupt things for the better. Remember - you will get better at this but you will never perfect it.

12
Data-Driven Innovation

A large part of any innovative idea is to get past the burden of proof and maneuvering through the skeptical push-back you'll get not only from your own nagging thoughts, but from the individuals you'll be in front of to move your concept forward. Oftentimes, it's a combination of the research you pull together, a little luck, a great deal of networking, and whatever ability you have to sell, that makes the case. Given the level of sophistication in today's society around the use of data, an individual has limitless potential to leverage data and information to transform their creative ideas and concepts into something meaningful even before it gets off the starting line.

A man steps out into the street to walk over to a flower hut each day, smells the fresh flowers, reads the newspaper, then walks three blocks south to the same coffee shop and orders the same cup of coffee before walking two more blocks south to his office. He steps out at noon to attend a business lunch every once in awhile, but other than that he pretty much eats at his desk for lunch spending his time surfing the internet.

Given that narrative, in what ways could you make his life easier? What other information would you need to figure out in order for you to present your concept in such a way that he will clearly see the value? Are there conclusions you could draw from this on how you could make his life better? The problem with data-driven anything, is that you'll always be working with an incomplete picture. The confidence gap will be larger or smaller, depending on the data you're working with, and what you're building your conclusions on; and there will always be more information that would be helpful to have. Other pieces of information are obvious or meaningless depending on what you're attempting to solve. For instance, knowing the man liked smelling flowers at the flower shop would only help you in innovating certain types of concepts that would appeal to him such as new scents or flower stores, but not help with emissions testing or improving the life of computer monitors.

In any given context, for any given idea, you have more information at your fingertips than you could possibly have time to process. From private data within your company that you can mine via your corporate intranet to public census data that you could find at data.gov and query. There you could pull data to predict what may be popular all the way over to monitoring the outcomes of a new concept and fine-tune the solution based on the sales statistics combined with third-party data to give you added context about why markets react the way they do.

To be innovative in an entirely new way, thinking outside the box and following the steps I've discussed in this book will go a long way in helping you work through the hurdles that people face in a typical company when it comes to launching new initiatives. It will also create the kind of stickiness and resilience that will transform you into a true innovator. However, the biggest weapon you have on your side will be the effective use of data, and how you leverage it to surround every aspect of your concept. When people encounter a new frontier, the first people to successfully map and claim the valuable resources are the ones to grow the richest from that frontier, and in turn influence everything else that happens around them. Within the last several years, more books and tools have been released giving people the ability to map, plot, sort, and leverage the data frontier that it's become a land grab in every direction to see who can take advantage of what the fastest.

In this data frontier is gold buried under the rubble that not only gives you context into what the flower-smelling man really would be interested in buying, but also what he'd be most interested in getting the three closest people around him to buy as well, and then convincing five to eight people in his office to back and support an innovative new concept that he would have some small part in. Though data isn't a silver bullet, it could give you more than a fifty-fifty shot at figuring out what you will need to build a more successful widget, get your concept out the door, and gain the support of the folks needed to back that concept. With the right data, you'll win more than you lose and end up ahead of the game along the way - even when you encounter the occasional failure as you go.

Working for a large corporation as a consultant some years back, I was tasked with taking several different data sources and fishing out a simple question - Is this division of the business profitable or not? Thousands of employees, millions of records, tens of millions of data points, and a simple question couldn't surface the data to determine the cost of the solution in a handful of simple words. It turned out this business had used several different methods for determining this answer in the past, all were more or less accurate, but since the number differed there was a need to come up with a single version of the truth. This led to massive overhauls, several meetings, and several dozen groups of consultants being hired to help get to the bottom of this single answer and once and for all determine the one true number that would tie to the revenue, and help serve as a useful tool on an executive dashboard to trend out how the business unit was doing and what needed to be done to either grow it, maintain it, or emulate it elsewhere.

After several months of work, and wrangling hundreds of different types of data we had an answer, but ended up needing yet another method for how the figure was calculated to be able to stand side by side with prior results because our method took the data in a new enough direction that there was no "apples to apples" method for comparing historic results. What it came down to was process and politics; simplicity over complexity was needed, but was convoluted by adding more complexity to try and get there. If we'd eliminated all those systems, overhauled the solution, and started from scratch, we could have had a cleaner system with better data going back to the beginning and a more efficient method for calculating the key metrics.

The Lesson here? Have the discernment to know when to cut your losses on leveraging data. Avoid focusing too much on individual data points and thereby miss the fact that a system that's too complex to track its cost is probably too complex to really be profitable down the road. Don't spend all your time just trying to get that single number to show you what stepping back and looking down at the macro-level could easily indicate.

You don't need complex data analysis to determine what is sometimes obvious; heed this as a word of warning, when it comes to leveraging data, if you're too far down into the weeds, you will miss the obvious.

Also keep in mind that sometimes the best product in the world will lose to better marketing, and the best data and best numbers in the world will lose because someone else had a more convincing PowerPoint. As useful as data is, it's yet another tool in the toolbox that should be wielded and understood, but kept in the right context so it's not data alone that you're using to base your concept.

Most importantly though, don't use data as a crutch or to simply justify what you are already thinking. Sometimes it can reveal something you don't want to believe, and can also sometimes be wrong, so don't believe all data blindly. Heck, you may even have calculated something incorrectly along the way, so hold it loosely while respecting it and leverage it to find insights you normally wouldn't find as you begin to separate the trees from the forest. You can extract those resources from the frontier and gain valuable tools not just for moving your concept forward, but also to aid you with every step in the innovative process.

13
Models for Insight

In this chapter, we will explore some models that I have used at various points to help communicate the concepts and best practices we have discussed in this book. The goal here is to help articulate the discussion for those who are more visually minded, and give you some ways to start the conversation using a white board. Then you can have a discussion with your own team to bring some of this work to life. If it stays in the book, it will have no real impact on your day-to-day life. Bringing this to life means finding a way to immediately turn around and create something useful that your team will use and put into practice. These are basic black and white drawings because it is cheaper to print in B&W, and it makes them easier for you to duplicate them on the white board. If you want more description, or color, head to http://www.buildingtheexpo.com and download the models in greater detail as well as get some whitepapers and additional information on the concepts outlined in this book.

Begin by drawing the following diagram on the white board and adding a handful of notes about how this model is relevant to you, and the concept you are working on. Take a picture of the white board and store it in your favorite note taking app (Evernote, OneNote, etc.) then find one to three articles that discuss the context you used to make this model relevant to you. Find a couple of appropriate quotes, and then put the whole thing on a one-page paper with the model at the top along with proper citation. File this in a digital or physical notebook to pull up and reference again for a business plan or presentation. This is a helpful exercise if you are not used to taking something you have in front of you, building a context around it, adding relevant third party input, and focusing on re-use and reference management. Next pull out the models, and see if you can use at least one or two in a meeting with the references fresh in your mind so you can build a quick five to ten minute story around what it is you are discussing. You will be surprised how the dots will connect when creating your own models to describe your concept and establishing a new context for innovation to effectively grow from. As Clayton Christenson stated in the "*Innovator's DNA*", "Put simply, innovative thinkers connect fields, problems, or ideas that others find unrelated.4"

Model 1: Use Cases Through Situation, Role and Task

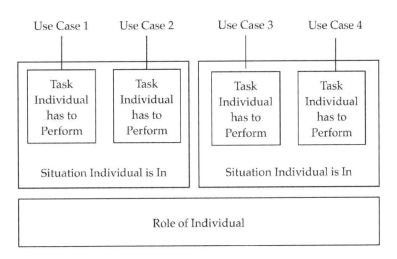

When thinking through the use cases in the initial ideation of a concept, it is important to put the concept in the right context of the individual and understand how it will be utilized by them. Even if you are building a widget where one system will interact with another, someone will have to write the check and will need to understand the value.

Building a story around the value proposition using the situation the protagonist might be in, along with the role of the individual, and the task they are undertaking within the context of this concept, will help to frame early on how likely someone is to not only understand the value but buy in.

Model 2: Usability through Consumption, Production, and Interaction

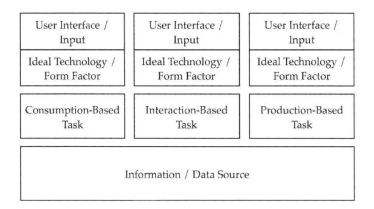

With new gadgets continually being released, it is incredibly easy to get caught up in finding the right device for the job, and in how it will be released and used by employees at your company. There is a strong focus on software development to spend more time understanding the interface and interaction, and less around the back-end engineering. With the growth of cloud-enabled mobile services and the level of automation and intelligence focused around web services, there is a greater need to understand more of the individual and what they will be doing, so you can engineer around the use case and worry about the specifics of the solution later.

Focusing on whether someone is consuming content, producing content, or interacting with content will help to quickly determine what is ideal from a form factor and input standpoint, as well as incorporating the situation, role and task for the use case in which they will typically be interfacing with the concept. This not only applies to software development, but can apply to anything from a new way to bind and print books for people on the go to a unique way to engineer bikes for those that have much to accomplish while they are bike riding. Transactions can occur on all three, and a device optimized for one does not mean you cannot use it for the other two. The goal is to get to the ideal form factor, and think about how an application built for the input tools on a computer, for example, might not transfer well to a touch-based smart phone with one quarter the size of screen. There are hundreds of ways to break up this model and they can be added to or changed, but this gives you a starting point that you can evolve as you think of new ways to break down tasks into form factors and interfaces.

Model 3: Hierarchy of Expertise

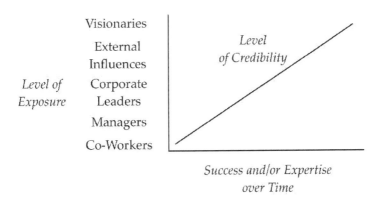

Having a clear sense of how to build a brand is important to elevating what it is you are producing or saying, from anecdotal input to market-shifting commentary. Some people have the power to command the masses with a single tweet, and others can write numerous blogs without a single response. It is important to know where you are in your level of influence and how you can elevate the brand in the process of developing the concept.

It is a vital part in gaining sponsorship, and should not be dismissed as purely an internal pursuit. Getting other's input about brand building within an enterprise means you can discuss what approach might be most effective and what types of methods you can use to maneuver through the concept development. What level do you need to be at to get executive sponsorship? How about a meeting with the CEO? Is now the right time to push for a large-scale concept, or do you need some quick wins to build the reputation to try and get something bigger funded?

Perhaps there's internal projects you can support, or get recognized outside the company as a thought leader by speaking at local events or going through official channels to get published for insights you have around the concept you are thinking about? Being strategic and planning on how much how soon can make all the difference on making big things happen. However, do not be afraid to move faster if you are not getting any traction. It may involve risk, so know how much time to spend building and how much time to spend pushing.

Model 4: A Maturity Model for Trend

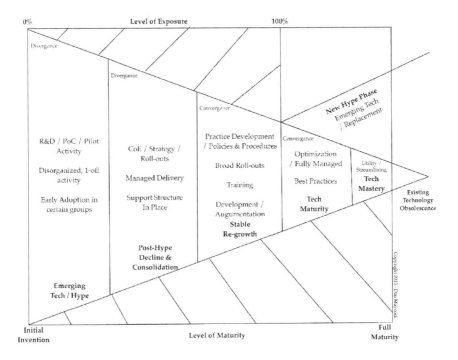

There are many models out there around hype, innovation, and product maturity, but none really hit on areas like exposure and the impact of the next trend on the existing one. So I've have developed this model to help illustrate some of the factors that will affect the technology trend apart from what phase it's in. Consider mapping technologies from other models onto this one, and see what insights you might be able to gain beyond what you already have been considering. Then bring others into the conversation to get their impressions, and understand the impact on the concept you are thinking about and if it is too early or late to really make some headway in the company. For example, is this a good time to leverage the hype over a new trend to propel your concept forward?

Much like sandwiching medicine inside peanut butter and

jelly can help medicine go down easier, attaching a risky or unproven concept in with a well hyped trend can help gain stronger support from skeptics.

Model 5: GUIDE Model

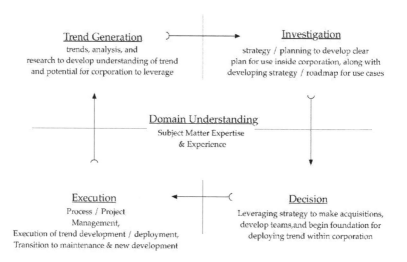

When it comes to incorporating new ideas into a company, the concept has a lifecycle that works its way from being introduced as a trend to having a project build and launched focused on that concept taking root in the organization. Consider different concepts in your company, and map them to which box they belong in. Is the idea something you are seeing for the first time? Or has it been build and implemented, with a focus on efficiency and execution? Having mastery of each of these phases can demonstrate domain expertise in that area, and help build your credibility when talking about new ideas. Are you looking to incorporate innovative new mobile ideas? Consider where concepts like mobile payments are versus where heads up displays and Google glasses sit versus mobile applications.

Model 6 - Hierarchy of Use

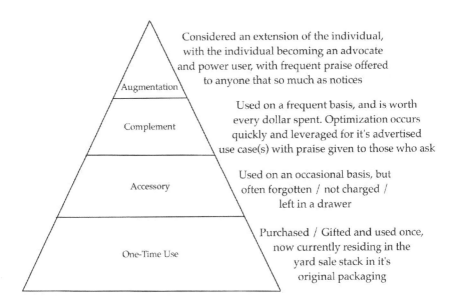

All because an idea is well known does not necessarily mean it is popular or frequently used, and there is a strong difference between useful technology and drawer fodder as far as enterprise sentiment goes. Saying any technology is useful technology does not apply to stakeholders and teammates, so having a clear idea of where you are and where you are working to be is important in understanding how useful the concept will be over time.

14
The Power of a Brand

Building a brand is difficult in today's society. Just about everyone seems to be posting material online, writing blogs or posting on Facebook pages, yet few are changing the world in drastic and well publicized ways. It often takes years of hard work to make positive contributions on a large scale. In today's world it is even more difficult to find a way to stand out enough to attract people's attention, and gain their support to push the envelope to get your disruptive concepts out there in the enterprise.

The payoff for putting yourself out there isn't guaranteed. In the story at the beginning of the book, Mack was assigned the task of building an innovative product, and ran into a number of issues common in most corporations. So how do you get from where you are, to where you want to be? How do you begin such a journey? Keeping a job, working toward a promotion, saving up enough for the family vacations, and keeping a rhythm in your home-life while not overworking is a noble pursuit, and something many people strive for in their lifetime. Those who do not keep a good balance between pursuing professional growth and maintaining a healthy personal life will lose sight of their purpose on this earth. If you feel all you are here to do is clock in and out, prepare dinner, attend your kids' games, and prepare for retirement, then you are ignoring what makes you unique.

Not all of us are trailblazers, but each of us has a purpose outside of just keeping the lights on. You would be surprised how many of the things you have to do can be done more efficiently so you can start to think about what you want to do by simply learning a more effective strategy. First, figure out what it is you really want to do and really desire to contribute. Then, gain the support of those around you to accomplish it.

Any innovation requires people buying-off and believing in you or your concept to move it forward. If you are someone that just is not cut out for innovating and crafting the idea from scratch, consider what you can bring to the table. For every person that loves to come up with new ideas, there must be someone who is willing to take the idea and act on it. For every one person that likes to act on ideas, there needs to be someone who is willing to maintain the innovation. Each type of skill set plays a pivotal role in the grand scheme of making a disruptive concept take light, whether it is a start-up or an enterprise.

Regardless of what it is you bring to the table, and what your role is in making innovation happen, it is important you have a brand so people know who you are. Standing up does not necessarily mean standing out. It will take some effort on your part to rise above the noise to put out a distinct signal letting people around you know what it is you do best. There are millions of blogs out there describing everything from what types of food people eat to how their dogs look dressed in human clothes. Figure out what it is you are most passionate about, and begin to publish it online. Having a brand does not require spending hours promoting it to the world. However, it's important to have something online for people to get a sense of who you are and a context for what it is you are good at beyond what your resume says. Context and positioning through posting passions online gives people that have heard about you something to look into, and creates an icebreaker that makes it easier for whoever is leading the initiative to place you appropriately. Are you leading the pack, and driving the concepts to stakeholders? It is even more important you have something you are contributing to regularly because branding internally and externally demonstrates that this is not a passing fancy for you. You do not have to blog, you can journal and keep the material handy so you have something you can share if asked. This will help people establish a brand around you. Keeping a strong presence on social media networks, such as LinkedIn or Facebook, can help provide more insight, as well as network, but you decide what kind of brand it is you really want, and what it is you want to be associated with. There are a number of resources online today, you can find several just by googling "Online Branding," but I highly recommend starting with one network, like LinkedIn, to focus your time and attention and then continue to branch out from there as other social networks make sense for you to engage with.

To be recognized both internally and externally in your company as someone that has powerful ideas that can really change things means building a brand as a thought leader. This is aimed specifically at those that want to get out there in the world of online publications, journals, and public speaking. Each company has rules and standards, some of which require you to be established before receiving the go ahead to participate as a thought leader outside the company, but each company in today's world has avenues inside the company as well the ability to demonstrate thought leadership. If you are an engineer that wants to be an interior decorator, ask about attending building management meetings and speaking about thoughts you have to make the offices more aesthetically productive. If you are an accountant that wants to get into cloud computing, get to know an IT executive and do the hard work to become trained or certified in cloud computing and offer to spend lunches being mentored, or contribute off hours to projects in the cloud space that you can apply your training to.

What can also help is publishing material externally on your own, that doesn't reference the company, and simply discussing passions you have that demonstrate you know what you are talking about. Internally, when it comes time to meeting with people whom you want to work with, work for, or approach for sponsorship, having a brand, as a thought leader in the space will help.

Where Does One Begin in Becoming a Thought Leader?

The first step to becoming a thought leader is to establish a theme. If you do not know what you want your brand to be, you should sit down and develop a personal value proposition to determine what you have a passion for, and how you want to impact your audience, career, and goals with your brand. You can certainly change course along the way, but to be effective you need to have a focus so people start to align your subject matter with your expertise. If you have a strong passion for gardening, for example, but tweet pictures of cats and post articles on Facebook about your favorite foods, then it will be difficult for people to identify you as someone with a green thumb.

It is important to be well rounded, but you should think about how everything you share online and off represents you and your brand. Your theme should be focused around what you want to achieve professionally, and maybe even personally, because it will take work and dedication to cut through the noise and create the type of signal people want to tune into.

Once you have a clear idea about the brand you want to build and the strengths you bring to the table, create three to four topics to focus on. It helps if they are related, as the broader the topics, the more difficult it will be for your community to connect with you as an influencer. If you want to become an expert on mobility, for example, it would make more sense to focus on smartphones, mobile apps and mobile payments to build credibility than it would to focus on wireless transmission, global supply-chain logistics, or social networking. The latter three topics do have tie-ins to mobile technology but are topics in and of themselves.

People look to experts who are the best in their field. If you are too broad, you may come across as a jack-of-all-trades and master-of-none. Sharing timely, unique insights people cannot get anywhere else will help you gain recognition as an expert in your field.

Take Your Topics and Build a News Feed

Once you have identified the topics you want to focus on, the next step is to do your research via reliable sources of information. These could be anything from RSS feeds to folks on Twitter you may want to follow. If you are completely new to the topic, start by understanding the foundational works in the field. Who first discussed the topic? Who are the big influencers in the field? To begin, you can head to Google Reader and search for academic papers written on your topics. Although they tend to not be the most exciting reads, foundational works are often cited in the bibliographies. If you see the same book cited three to four times in multiple papers, it is a good indicator that book is worth checking out. Getting grounded, at least on a theoretical level, helps provide context that gives you insight into posts relating to the topic at hand and allows you to contribute your own thoughts more quickly.

Once you feel comfortable with the fundamentals of your topic, have a good understanding of the terminology, and of who's who in the industry, you can begin to filter through the daily information feeds and select the ones you want to stay up-to-date on. Mixing up the mediums of your sources is important as well-meaning you are not just reading blogs, but also consuming a handful of books, podcasts, RSS feeds, and other subject-matter material that will help you remain grounded and give you a strong sense of the industry at large.

Keeping an eye on the movers and shakers in your area of expertise is also important. While you don't need to become an investment broker, developing a clear sense of how the big guys are doing and how things like mergers or bankruptcies would shake up the industry is important. For example, If you are a baseball expert, you probably have a handful of teams you know really well, but you also follow the draft and have at least a working understanding of how players coming and going will impact the season overall. It does not mean you have to have every player committed to memory, but knowing the stats of a player when it comes up on ESPN will give you a sense of why the player is newsworthy. This is no different than following the mobility industry well enough to know how Google buying Motorola will impact the mobile landscape.

Take Your News Feed and Build a Following

Once you have identified key resources and are up to date on the latest information about your topic, you will be able to not only comment on what you are reading, but have a sense of where things are heading. Depending on the topic, this may take a while, to be able to predict changing tides in the industry, but you should be able to see how one piece of news relates to another and comment about why it is important for readers to pay attention. The key thing to keep in mind is that not everyone has the grounding on the topic that you do, so bring your commentary up a couple levels. That way, those who know nothing about your topic can understand how it relates to them.

Deep levels of detail may appeal to hardcore enthusiasts, but the average person will spend thirty seconds skimming your article, and then move on to the next one if it doesn't grab his or her attention. Save the deep-level talks for conferences, and use lists or 5x5 essays to sum up your thoughts in a way that is easy to consume and pass along.

Once you begin to be seen as a thought leader who can articulate thoughts and share knowledge through a variety of mediums, your content will begin to be passed around and shared. You can track how well this is going by using a number of different tools, such as Google Analytics for your blog, and Sprout Social, or Hootsuite for your Twitter, LinkedIn, and Facebook accounts. There are a number of methods to help you build your community; keeping things to the point and giving people the right amount of information is a solid way to organically build a steady stream of followers.

If it is a topic you are passionate about, you will not have a hard time staying current. If you find it is hard to stay up to date, you might want to reconsider the topic you have chosen to pursue. Consider how much content you want to write on your own versus how much content you want to cite and share. Though sharing or re-tweeting content from influential people is a good way to build up followers, you need to contribute your own content to be identified as someone with something new and unique to share.

Consistency and discipline are critical to any successful brand. There are tools available to help you schedule tweets. If you have an hour every day to read up on your topics, spread out your messages so you can share a steady stream of content on all your major networks. It is also helpful to join topic-related groups on LinkedIn and follow companies in your industry on Twitter. It's a quick way for someone scanning your profile to see what areas you self-identify with and perhaps have influence on. What matters most, though, is that you are regularly contributing to your feeds. If you have not posted on your blog in six months, ask yourself how realistic it is to keep your blog updated versus contributing through other mediums, such as LinkedIn groups. Stale content shows a lack of time and, more importantly, can indicate a lack of interest. People make time for their passions, which does not mean just your topic, but also your passion about being a thought leader and contributing to the larger conversations concerning your topic.

Take Your Following, and Build a Brand

Once you have a good following of people, are contributing actively to communities, and have built a consistent image between your social networks and websites, it is time to take it to the next level. If you have a strong pipeline of followers and have developed consistent messaging, consider how you want to elevate your contributions to influence the influencers. Writing blogs will only get you so far, but creating whitepapers or other documents to demonstrate expertise in the form of a two to three page topic paper along with applying to speak at conferences about your topic will help you gain recognition as a thought leader that people want to hear from.

Write whitepapers and topical papers on an issue related to your topic, and make them available for download through your website. This is a great way to expand from writing 300-500 words on a topic, not only demonstrating your ability to share complex information at a consumable level, but also helping to prepare you for writing longer pieces - maybe even an e-book or non-fiction book. Although writing books is not essential for being seen as a thought leader, it can help get your name known.

Most conferences accept applications for speakers - you can find applications on the conference websites. Even if you are not selected to speak, pick two to three conferences throughout the year you want to participate in, as this is essential to building up your network as you grow in your level of influence. If you cannot get permission to speak, attend as a participant. If you are unable to obtain permission from your company to go, consider taking a vacation somewhere nearby and attend it out of your own pocket. Remember, passion will make up for ability as you are getting started, so consider this part of bootstrapping.

If you work *for* a company, then you are part of that company's culture and your identity is intertwined. If you work *at* a company, you are an individual working as a free agent, like someone that will not commit to a baseball team regardless of how the team does. The truth is that it's very hard to make a living out of building your own brand, as it is a full-time job for people who do it really well. If you have a job as a consultant, employee, or manager, you can only help yourself by helping to promote the company through your own interests and topics. No one rises to the top of the thought-leader pile on their own, and most people with strong brands got their start by first making the companies where they worked look good. Eventually, they were promoted to higher levels of influence, and then used that influence to make their mark more visible.

It boils down to whether you have an attitude of working

at a company or of working for a company. Even if you are not 100% sold on sticking with the company you are at currently, you will only help yourself by taking an active role in opportunities to showcase and demonstrate your knowledge within the company circles. It is also seen as a strong networking asset to associate yourself with a well-known brand, as it will help you gain credibility faster than you could on your own. You will find that sharing your insights through company channels will not only help you build your own brand internally, but will also help you be noticed externally and grow your career through greater exposure and influence.

Consider what avenues your company has for people to contribute their thought leadership to the company, and how that can help you in the role you are in now. Having your company's weight behind you will only lead to good things down the road, as your brand will go with you no matter where your career leads.

Free agents still swing for the fence to help their teams win the World Series because holding back from the team not only hurts their record, but will keep the team itself from getting noticed and hurt the player's chances of being recruited elsewhere. Whether you are all in or not, a World Series win is always a good thing. Helping your team win will also make you more valuable to the team itself, allowing you to not only establish a good foothold in the company, but also build your chances for promotions and greater job opportunities.

The keys to becoming a thought leader and having a strong brand are consistency, patience, and tenacity. If you flip-flop on your interests too often, it will be very hard to keep people engaged enough to stick with you. If you drop off the radar, and stop contributing, you will lose your following to greener pastures. It will take some time to build up a steady community with active and useful contributions to your content, but once you have hit enough conferences and blogs, people will begin seeking out your contributions to magazines, online journals, and other forums. This will in turn help you elicit speaking engagements that can build your brand and influence around your area of expertise.

The competition is huge, but by simply keeping a consistent presence and actively contributing to the larger conversations on topic blogs, forums, and conferences, you will outlast 95% of the people posting similar content. Through the information and tips in this book, you can rise to the top of the crowd and become a thought leader in your area of passion and expertise.

Afterword

My goal in putting this book together was to advance the ongoing discussion around methods and strategies for bringing innovation to the workplace. The principles outlined here are based on firsthand accounts of implementing new concepts at several different Fortune 500 companies, and takes an honest look at when things have gone well and not so well in the innovation process in order to help you, the reader, build a successful process for bringing your own concepts and ideas into reality. Too many works written on the topic paint the picture for bringing about innovation in theory, without talking about the techniques or the difficulties in building your own process within your own unique environment. In writing this book, and sharing the concepts with people, it became clear there would be a second book written from the standpoint of taking this content and discussing how to replicate this approach inside groups throughout a company versus keeping the process isolated into a single unrepeatable silo. It's one thing to build a new process once, but entirely another thing to then take that process and reproduce success in a new situation or department within the company.

It takes an entirely different set of skills and processes to make something successful happen in multiple groups throughout a company in order to reproduce that innovative best practice in a hundred different teams. If we look at the first chapter of Sun Tzu's "*Art of War* 1", Master Tzu discusses the five things that will make for a victory in war. "*Building The Expo*" is meant to help you understand the first three principles. The first principle, the moral law, is all about how to cause people to follow you in complete accord regardless of the personal impact. In war, this of course looks very different than it does in business, but user buy-in from your co-workers, leaders, and employees is paramount to being successful as an innovator. The second principle, heaven, discusses the environment you're operating within. The principle applies to whether high or low ground makes a difference, the effect of rain on the battlefield, etc. For this context, the culture and makeup of your company will have a big impact on how you can approach launching an innovative idea and how you can take your surroundings into account when it comes to getting buy-off and moving an idea through the risk-based immune system within a company. The third principle, earth, discusses aspects such as the terrain, taking into account the hardness of the ground, distances to travel, etc. In this context, it's important to consider aspects such as whether you work for a multi-national company versus a start-up and the realities of regulations and reporting structures that make up the sometimes overly rigid structures that keep truly innovative ideas from springing up.

There has been a lot written about being innovative, and creating a series of steps on how to grow ideas into products, but a lot of literature doesn't take the realities of enterprises into account and the hurdles the typical employee or manager will run into. These first three principles begin to describe the difficulty you'll likely encounter, and provide a process to build innovative idea #1. The key that will be addressed in the following book though, is replicating that success as an executive or senior leader throughout multiple departments within a company, and not just once within a particular group.

The fourth principle Master Tzu discusses, the commander, is all about your beliefs, values, and models making up the integrity and core of a leader. This is important to the success of replicating your innovative process, because being an innovator is something that can be taught and learned, but each individual comes with their own pretext and a sub-culture that can come with it's own challenges. Training teams and raising leaders to command new ideas is the key to successful replication, and will help a new concept work it's way through that organization without you having to micromanage or handhold the individual you're recruiting to play a key role in spreading that innovative best practice.

The fifth principle, method & discipline, is all about the organization of troops and using goals to help them focus on outcomes in battle despite the chaos that exists within large groups of soldiers as the fight commences and battles erupt. In business, you can only control so many variables, and the real key to war is to win before you go to battle. Defeating the opponent in this case means going to war with everything from apathy, to a lack of discipline, to fear around risky investments. Having clear methods and disciplines in place means that everyone is equipped and adaptable, despite the issues that can sideline progress and cause people to panic either due to macro-economic factors (i.e. the stock price drops due to unusually bad weather and your project is at risk of being cut) or internal issues such as a massive re-org or change in leadership.

Being innovative as a company is much harder than having an innovation team, but it's the key to truly making an impact in the long run and help your company be successful. From changing the culture, to accepting higher levels of risk, the path isn't an easy one but it'll ensure your company remains proactive, and stays far ahead of your competitors for years to come.

I hope you found this book valuable, and am anticipating sharing my next book with you, which will explore the ideas above in much greater detail. Until then I look forward to hearing from you online (Twitter Name: @DanMaycock). I encourage you to reach out and let me know how your efforts to implement innovative processes on your current projects are going. I'd be happy to be a resource and walk alongside you as we explore how to take these best practices and begin spreading them to every part of your company.

About The Author

Daniel Maycock resides in Seattle, WA with his family where he works to help make companies more successful through the use of data-driven solutions and innovation best practices as a Senior Manager at Capgemini.

You can find Dan on Twitter at @DanMaycock or on LinkedIn at http://www.linkedin.com/in/danmaycock

Bibliography

1. Anthony, Scott. The Little Black Book of Innovation: How It Works, How to Do It. Boston: Harvard Business Review, 2012.

2. Bahrami, Homa, and Stuart Evans. Super-flexibility for Knowledge Enterprises. Berlin: Springer, 2005.

3. Christensen, Clayton M. The Innovator's Dilemma: When New Technologies Cause Great Firms to Fail - Boston: Harvard Business School Press, 1997.

4. Christensen, Clayton M., Jeff Dyer and Hal Gregersen. The Innovator's DNA: Mastering the Five Skills of Disruptive Innovators. Harvard Business Review Press, 2011.

5. Denning, Peter. Dunham, Robert. The Innovator's Way: Essential Practices for Successful Innovation. Cambridge: MIT Press, 2010.

6. Innovate. Dictionary.com. Dictionary.com Unabridged. Random House, Inc. http://dictionary.reference.com/browse/innovate. (accessed: September 05, 2013).

7. Field of Dreams. Universal. 1989. Videocassette.

8. Leonard, George. Mastery: The Keys to Success and Long-Term Fulfillment. New York: Plume, Reissue Edition, 1

A Special Thanks to
My Kickstarter Supporters

Jeff Barber

Hunter Barcello

Dan Bittner

Veronica Bittner

David Campbell

Garret Carlson

Brett Dillahunt

Craig Dupler

Travis Fine

Rex Foxford

Gabe Geise

John Garrett

Steve Isley

Erik Johnson

Scott Johnston

Roger Kastner

Matthew Kennedy

Mike King

Christina Maiers

Caitlin Escobar

Cindy Maycock

Frank Maycock

Steve Maycock

Duncan McDougall

Kevin McKay

Thomas Osborn

Tim Oten

Loretta Pain

Rodrigo Perez

Erik Pierson

Maurice Ramsey

Sean Richter

Todd Rubie

Jeff Rubingh

Nicola Russell

David & Kendra Uhler

Jarek Wilkiewicz

Mark Zocher

Made in the USA
San Bernardino, CA
15 September 2015